GEOMETRIC DESIGN PRACTICES FOR EUROPEAN ROADS

PREPARED BY THE STUDY TOUR TEAM

Jim Brewer
Kansas DOT

John German
City of San Antonio

Ray Krammes
FHWA

Kam Movassaghi
Louisiana DOT

John Okamoto
Washington DOT

Sandra Otto
FHWA

Wendell Ruff
Mississippi DOT

Seppo Sillan
FHWA

Nikiforos Stamatiadis
University of Kentucky

Robert Walters
Arkansas DOT

American Trade Initiatives, Inc.
&
Avalon Integrated Services, Inc.

for the

Federal Highway Administration
U.S. Department of Transportation

and

The American Association of State Highway and
Transportation Officials

and

The National Cooperative Highway Research Program
(Panel 20-36)
of the Transportation Research Board

June 2001

Technical Report Documentation Page

1. Report No. FHWA-PL-01-026	2. Government Accession No.	3. Recipient's Catalog No.
4. Title and Subtitle Geometric Design Practices for European Roads		5. Report Date June 2001
		6. Performing Organization Code
7. Author(s) Jim Brewer, John German, Ray Krammes, Kam Movassaghi, John Okamoto, Sandra Otto, Wendell Ruff, Seppo Sillan, Nikiforos Stamatiadis, Robert Walters		8. Performing Organization Report No.
9. Performing Organization Name and Address American Trade Initiatives P.O. Box 8228 Alexandria, VA 22306-8228		10. Work Unit No.(TRAIS)
		11. Contract or Grant No. DTFH61-99-C-0005
12. Sponsoring Agency Name and Address Office of International Programs Office of Policy Federal Highway Administration U.S. Department of Transportation		13. Type of Report and Period Covered
		14. Sponsoring Agency Code

15. Supplementary Notes
FHWA COTR: Donald W. Symmes, Office of International Programs

16. Abstract
The objective of the scanning tour was to review and document European procedures and practices in roadway geometric design and context-sensitive design, in which a balance is sought between safety and mobility needs and community interests. The U.S. group visited sites in Sweden, Denmark, the Netherlands, England, and Germany, and met with numerous representatives from transportation and highway ministries, research organizations, and consultants.

In the European countries, the general philosophy for highway design and project development is to develop a transportation program and system that enhances community values and integrates roadways into communities and the environment. This philosophy is supported by very high safety goals.

The U.S. delegation found potentially transferable practices regarding public involvement in project planning; self-explaining, self-enforcing rural roads; design flexibility; area-wide traffic calming measures; intersection control through roundabouts; and integration of bicyclists and pedestrians.

17. Key Words Context-sensitive design, traffic calming, roundabout, self-explaining, self-enforcing roads	18. Distribution Statement No restrictions. This document is available to the public from the Office of International Programs FHWA-HPIP, Room 3325 U.S. Dept. of Transportation Washington, DC 20590 international@fhwa.dot.gov www.international.fhwa.dot.gov

19. Security Classif. (of this report) Unclassified	20. Security Classif. (of this page) Unclassified	21. No. of Pages 60	22. Price Free

Form DOT F 1700.7 (8-72)   Reproduction of completed page authorized

FHWA INTERNATIONAL TECHNOLOGY EXCHANGE PROGRAMS

The FHWA's international programs focus on meeting the growing demands of its partners at the Federal, State, and local levels for access to information on state-of-the-art technology and the best practices used worldwide. While the FHWA is considered a world leader in highway transportation, the domestic highway community is very interested in the advanced technologies being developed by other countries, as well as innovative organizational and financing techniques used by the FHWA's international counterparts.

INTERNATIONAL TECHNOLOGY SCANNING PROGRAM

The International Technology Scanning Program accesses and evaluates foreign technologies and innovations that could significantly benefit U.S. highway transportation systems. Access to foreign innovations is strengthened by U.S. participation in the technical committees of international highway organizations and through bilateral technical exchange agreements with selected nations. The program has undertaken cooperatives with the American Association of State Highway Transportation Officials and its Select Committee on International Activities, and the Transportation Research Board's National Highway Research Cooperative Program (Panel 20-36), the private sector, and academia.

Priority topic areas are jointly determined by the FHWA and its partners. Teams of specialists in the specific areas of expertise being investigated are formed and sent to countries where significant advances and innovations have been made in technology, management practices, organizational structure, program delivery, and financing. Teams usually include Federal and State highway officials, private sector and industry association representatives, as well as members of the academic community.

The FHWA has organized more than 40 of these reviews and disseminated results nationwide. Topics have encompassed pavements, bridge construction and maintenance, contracting, intermodal transport, organizational management, winter road maintenance, safety, intelligent transportation systems, planning, and policy. Findings are recommended for follow-up with further research and pilot or demonstration projects to verify adaptability to the United States. Information about the scan findings and results of pilot programs are then disseminated nationally to State and local highway transportation officials and the private sector for implementation.

This program has resulted in significant improvements and savings in road program technologies and practices throughout the United States, particularly in the areas of structures, pavements, safety, and winter road maintenance. Joint research and technology-sharing projects have also been launched with international counterparts, further conserving resources and advancing the state of the art.

For a complete list of International Technology Scanning topics, and to order free copies of the reports, please see the last page of this publication.

Website: www.international.fhwa.dot.gov
Email: international@fhwa.dot.gov

CONTENTS

EXECUTIVE SUMMARY

BACKGROUND

A properly designed roadway takes into consideration mobility and safety while addressing natural and human environmental aspects. To achieve such a balance, tradeoffs among these factors are needed and are routinely performed either explicitly or implicitly. Recently, an emphasis has been placed on the existing flexibility in design guidelines and the use of creative design in addressing the site-specific project needs has been encouraged. This philosophy was coined in the United States as context-sensitive design (CSD) and represents an approach in which a balance is sought between safety and mobility needs within the community interests. Both the Federal Highway Administration (FHWA) and the American Association of State Highway and Transportation Officials (AASHTO) recognize the flexibility that exists in the current design guidelines, while acknowledging that the current focus on providing high levels of mobility may conflict with some interests of the community. The use of multi-disciplinary teams and public involvement at the appropriate stages of the project are also aspects that promote the application of CSD. Research and workshops have increased awareness of CSD issues within the highway community and encouraged a desire to improve and enhance established roadway design practices and address elements of community interest.

> The objective of the scanning tour was to review and document European procedures and practices in roadway geometric design and context-sensitive design.

The CSD approach is a current practice in several European countries, which use these roadway geometric design concepts and tools to address mobility, safety, and community issues. From experience, European agencies may offer to U.S. practitioners valuable new insights and concepts on these issues and practices. Such concepts may be transferred or adapted to the U.S. environment to enhance the knowledge base regarding CSD and roadway geometric design.

The objective of the scanning tour was to review and document European procedures and practices in roadway geometric design and CSD. Sweden, Denmark, the Netherlands, England, and Germany were identified as countries that have innovative methods and procedures related to roadway geometric design and project development. The goal of the tour was to identify practices in the selected countries that, when implemented in the United States, would enhance current procedures and promote roadway designs that equally address mobility, safety, and community issues.

The International Scanning Tour for Roadway Geometric Design was jointly sponsored by FHWA and AASHTO, and the tour was coordinated by FHWA's Office of International Programs. The delegation included members representing FHWA, AASHTO, State departments of transportation (DOTs), the American Public Works Association (APWA), and academia. Individual team members brought their expertise in many roadway design and project developments areas, including CSD practices and procedures, application of geometric design principles for enhancing traffic safety and enforcing speed moderation, and consideration and integration of bicyclists and pedestrians in roadway design.

GENERAL CONCLUSIONS

The U.S. delegation met with numerous representatives from transportation and highway ministries, research organizations, and consultants, who shared many interesting ideas and insights with the scanning team. Practices that the delegation found most significant are summarized below.

Project Planning

The countries visited have an underlying philosophy of a project planning process that aims to improve safety yet remains sensitive to the needs of the community. The focus is on improving the existing system by making better use of it. All countries visited generally have project development processes similar to those in the United States; however, they devote a longer period of time to the planning process and consider longer sections, typically entire corridors. The Europeans also place greater emphasis on integrating projects in communities by addressing the public's concerns about speed management and aesthetics, particularly in urban areas.

In Europe, public involvement also is an integral part of the project development process, although degrees and levels of involvement vary on the basis of project type and country. Some concepts and methods to involve the public could be transferable to the United States and could help streamline existing practices. To avoid potential conflicts and problems after a project has been fully developed, all governments that the team met with stressed public involvement at the earliest stage possible.

Environmental Considerations

All the countries visited include environmental issues as an integral part of a project. It was interesting to find that several countries have copied or adapted the National Environmental Policy Act (NEPA) process, used in the United States, but have integrated it more efficiently within the project development process. The Dutch believe that recognition of environmental concerns is an everyday practice and that these concerns are addressed sufficiently through their normal design process. Currently, the Dutch are considering means by which the regulations and process can be streamlined to reduce project completion time. A general observation was that the highway agencies of the countries visited are more committed to addressing environmental issues than their U.S. counterparts; most of the issues presented were related to humans, including noise and concerns about historical preservation. The reliance on local governmental agencies to develop environmental impact studies (EIS) also was presented as a means of identifying problems and possible solutions more easily and at the local level.

Speeds

Although representatives from each country used different terms to describe their design speed, all use a guiding speed for designing roadways that ties the various roadway elements together. Roadway design philosophies common to all countries were the reliance on the physical roadway design to "enforce" operating speeds and the development of a "consistent" or "self-explaining" appearance for each road category. These self-explaining, self-enforcing roads are designed for specific purposes or functions. Safety is addressed in an efficient way, by implementing an aesthetic approach to explain the road function and enforce speeds. An interesting observation was that European road users accept lower operating speeds than users in the United States. This attitude may be attributable, in part, to a self-enforcing roadway design.

Design Flexibility

All countries visited utilize guidelines for roadway design that are considered central to the design philosophy, and all have a design exception process through which to address departures from guidelines. This process is more frequently applied to non-motorways (or non-freeways). It was also apparent that all these countries have or are currently revising their design guidelines, which are now more focused on addressing road purposes and creating a uniform appearance for each road category. This experience has encouraged an understanding of the value of design flexibility and exceptions. Generally, the countries are shielded from legal liability regarding design defects. The exception is England, where litigation generated by departures from design guidelines is expanding; most of the litigation is settled out of court. In the countries visited, the guidelines issued by the national highway authorities are usually considered to be recommendations for any projects under the authority of local governmental agencies. This provides great flexibility in designing to meet local needs and conditions.

Rural Roads

High speeds on rural roads is also a safety issue in the countries visited, and officials are focusing on attempts to control and reduce speeds. To achieve this objective, higher speeds are sacrificed to preserve safety. A common treatment on high-volume rural highways is 2+1 facilities, where the middle lane serves as a passing lane in which the right of way alternates. Use of this design instead of four-lane facilities has created gains in capacity and improvements in safety that may be transferable to the United States. Another approach for improving safety on these roads is the use of narrower lane widths, which requires drivers to slow down. This approach is implemented either by physically narrowing travelways or by visually decreasing the available roadway width. To further enforce the narrower roadway concept, clear zones are typically not provided, and some roadway objects are shielded by guardrails. It should be pointed out that such measures are only applied to non-motorways, where flexibility in design guidelines is permitted. On motorways, the guidelines are more rigid.

Traffic Calming

All countries are committed to reducing speeds through urban areas and are guided by the concept of integrating all modes and users in the same space. To achieve this objective, several traffic calming practices have been implemented in urban areas, including chicanes, islands, tables, cushions, humps, bumps, gates, landscaping, staggering, bollards, plantings, pavement textures and colors, and optical narrowing; i.e., narrowing the travelway with markings. For a successful implementation, an area-wide strategy is required, where a systemic, rather than localized, solution is sought. Thus the concept of traffic calming is enforced for the entire area, providing drivers with a clear and continuous message. Moreover, if roads are properly designed for the intended speed, drivers exceeding the speed are uncomfortable, but those traveling at the desired speed are not. Community acceptance is also very important for successful implementation. Most of these practices are transferable to the U.S. urban environment, although differences in land use, development, and transportation users must be recognized. In Europe, there appears to be greater public acceptance of reduced speed and mobility than in the United States.

Bicyclists and Pedestrians

All countries visited consider and address the needs of bicyclists and pedestrians, although there are two different philosophies regarding their levels of consideration. Sweden, Denmark, and the Netherlands place a high level of importance on addressing the needs of these users and provide separate facilities, as part of the network. Moreover, in those countries cycling and walking are heavily and systematically promoted as alternative transport modes. Germany and England, on the other hand, include these users in the planning process, but they are considered less important than in the other countries. One reason for the difference may be levels of demand, which are lower in Germany and England. All five countries place equal importance on the mobility needs of vehicles. One issue that all countries are struggling with is the integration of cyclists and pedestrians into roundabouts. Denmark and the Netherlands provide completely separate paths for these users, while other countries provide paths within the same travelway.

RECOMMENDATIONS AND IMPLEMENTATION STRATEGIES

In the European countries visited, the general philosophy for roadway design and project development is to develop a transportation program and system that enhances community values and integrates roadways into communities and the environment. This philosophy permeates the project development process, safety improvements, roadway design concepts, geometric design guidelines, public involvement, and environmental commitments. This philosophy is the essence of the recent emphasis on promoting the CSD approach in the United States. A shift toward this philosophy is supported by FHWA and many State DOTs. Moreover, the roadway design philosophy of the Europeans is to develop roadways designed for specific purposes, implement an aesthetic approach to visually explain the concepts, and address safety in a way that considers all users. Finally, all countries have very high safety goals (ranging from zero fatalities to reductions of more than 40 percent for all crashes) that guide the design approach and philosophy. To achieve the goals, planners are willing to provide roadways that self-enforce speed reductions, potentially increase levels of congestion, and promote alternative modes of transportation. This approach contrasts with the U.S. design philosophy, in which wider roads are deemed safer, there is heavier reliance on signs to communicate the intended message, and there is a lower tolerance for congestion and speed reduction.

While all practices are not entirely new to all U.S. States, lessons could be learned from the forms and extent of the applications in Europe. To this end, the U.S.

delegation identified a list of possible implementation strategies for enhancing existing project development and roadway geometric design practices in the United States.

Project Planning

While developing projects, State agencies may want to consider longer sections, to allow for a more systematic overview and definition of needs and deficiencies throughout the entire system. State and local agencies should, in urban areas, emphasize better integration of projects in communities by addressing the public's concerns about speed management and aesthetics. Public involvement, at the earliest possible stage of a project, is essential for a successful project, and this concept could be applied in the United States. Finally, the use of design workshops, in which all project alternatives are developed with public involvement, merits further examination, and could be transferable to U.S. practice.

Rural Roads

The concept of 2+1 roads has been shown to simultaneously address safety issues when addressing capacity on two-lane roadways. The practice requires further investigation for possible implementation in the United States, to determine specific design elements and guidelines. Self-explaining, self-enforcing roads are facilities designed for a specific purpose or function, and they address safety in an efficient way, for all users, by implementing an aesthetic approach to explain road function and enforce speed. Reliance on the roadway design to transmit its operating speed is integral to the concept, which contrasts with the higher reliance on traffic signs to convey speeds in the United States.

Traffic Calming

Traffic calming is an effective means of controlling speeds through urban areas and deserves wider implementation in the United States. Even though there are a variety of speed reduction levels, all studies completed indicate that, indeed, such devices reduce speeds. Traffic calming is most effective if done on a neighborhood or area-wide basis, and not just at spot locations. While some of the measures have been tried in the United States, to a limited degree, more testing of various European traffic calming strategies is needed in U.S. cities.

Roundabouts

Roundabouts are a very safe and efficient means of intersection control. Roundabouts with a single-lane approach are used widely and successfully in Europe, and they can easily accommodate peak flows of 2,500 vehicles per hour, without significant delays. Safety studies completed in most of the countries visited indicate that significant safety gains were achieved by implementing roundabouts instead of conventional intersections. Although roundabouts have been introduced in a few areas in the United States, this modern tool is still underutilized. State and local agencies should consider implementing and using roundabouts as an alternative to conventional intersection designs, as well as a means for improving traffic safety.

Bicyclists and Pedestrians

European countries place a significant emphasis on addressing the needs of pedestrians and bicyclists. In some countries, addressing the needs of these users is as important as improving vehicle mobility. Bicycle networks exist in all countries visited, and in some they are complete and rival the vehicle networks. In the United States, addressing mobility needs has been traditionally viewed as providing a roadway network where drivers can move as quickly and freely as they desire. This notion needs to be expanded to include all users, in order to address the safety needs of these vulnerable road users. State and local agencies are essential to promoting the use of these modes of transport and should focus on providing bicycle and pedestrian networks.

Context-Sensitive Design

The development of transportation projects and systems that enhance community values while integrating roadways into the environment is an everyday practice that all countries follow. Consideration is given to the desires and needs of the community by inviting the appropriate stakeholders to participate in the development of a project, thus influencing some of the solutions so they are acceptable to the community. This approach is currently promoted by FHWA and AASHTO, and it should be continued in the future, until CSD becomes an integral part of the design process in the United States. Although not unheard of in the United States, design solutions that reduce motor vehicle speeds or reduce the space available to drivers may increase trip times and are not often viewed as appropriate. But wider, high-speed roads that address only the mobility of automobiles may not meet the needs of other users of the transportation system and often encourage higher travel speeds that contribute to the greater severity of crashes. CSD implies a flexible application of the established geometric criteria in designing roadways. The use of innovative design to address local problems and provide solutions within the context of the area is essential to applying the CSD concept. The self-explaining, self-enforcing road is an example of such innovative design, because it encourages lower operating speeds for automobiles while incorporating safety and mobility for all transportation modes.

CHAPTER 1
INTRODUCTION

A properly designed roadway takes into consideration mobility and safety issues while addressing natural and human environmental aspects. To achieve such a balance, tradeoffs among these factors are routinely performed, either consciously or unconsciously. The passage of the Intermodal Surface Transportation Efficiency Act of 1991 (ISTEA) emphasized the importance of such roadway design. Practices that demonstrate such a design were compiled and documented in a report by the Federal Highway Administration (FHWA) titled *Flexibility in Highway Design*.[1] This document emphasized the existing flexibility in design criteria and encouraged the use of creative design in addressing site-specific project needs. Moreover, the need for project teams became apparent, because such creative solutions often require a cohesive effort among the planning, designing, and construction engineers. At the same time, the use of interdisciplinary teams and public involvement were also identified as integral components of successful solutions. This philosophy was coined in the United States as context-sensitive design (CSD) and represents an approach where a balance is sought between safety and mobility needs within the community interests. Both FHWA and the American Association of State Highway and Transportation Officials (AASHTO) recognize the flexibility that exists in the current design criteria, while acknowledging that the current focus on providing high levels of mobility may conflict with some community interests. There is increasing awareness of these CSD issues within the highway community; the Transportation Research Board (TRB) has initiated research to address CSD issues and several States have developed workshops. Moreover, there is a desire among the highway design community to improve roadway design practices and incorporate new elements to enhance established practices and address the community interest elements.

A properly designed roadway takes into consideration mobility and safety issues while addressing natural and human environmental aspects. To achieve such a balance, tradeoffs among these factors are routinely performed, either consciously or unconsciously.

The CSD approach is current practice in several European countries, which use these roadway geometric design concepts and tools to address mobility, safety, and community issues. Therefore, European agencies can offer the United States valuable new insights and concepts from their experience with these issues and practices. Such concepts can be transferred or adapted to the U.S. environment to enhance the knowledge base regarding CSD and roadway geometric design. Recognizing the potential benefits from examining such international practices, a team of engineers was formed to observe and document practices that might have value to U.S. practitioners. Sweden, Denmark, the Netherlands, England, and Germany were identified as countries with innovative methods and procedures related to roadway geometric design and project development. In June 2000 the team traveled to these countries and met with transportation officials to exchange ideas and document European practices. This report presents the findings of the scan tour and includes recommendations of practices that have potential for implementation in the United States.

TRIP OBJECTIVE

The objective of this scanning tour was to review and document procedures and practices in roadway geometric design and CSD in five European countries. The goal of the tour was to identify practices in these countries that, if implemented in the United States, would enhance current procedures and promote roadway designs that equally address mobility, safety, and community issues. The team's objective was to meet with representatives of transportation agencies in these countries, discuss their approach on these issues and, thus, understand and identify the possible similarities and differences between U.S. and European approaches to roadway geometric design and CSD. The team also wanted to observe applications of these concepts within the existing transportation system and gather information on examples of successful and not-so-successful applications to allow for a broader understanding of these issues. Therefore, a mixture was sought between team meetings and visits to sites where some of the concepts have been applied.

TRIP APPROACH

Panel Members

The International Scanning Tour for Roadway Geometric Design was jointly sponsored by FHWA and AASHTO, and the tour was coordinated by FHWA's Office of International Programs. American Trade Initiatives provided logistical support and guidance. The delegation included members representing FHWA, AASHTO, State departments of transportation (DOTs), the American Public Works Association (APWA), and academia. The delegation members offered expertise in many roadway geometric design and project development areas, including CSD practices and procedures, application and use of geometric design principles for enhancing traffic safety and enforcing speed moderation, and consideration and integration of bicyclists and pedestrians in roadway design. The team members and their affiliations are listed in Table 1, while a short biography of each member is included in Appendix A.

Table 1. Team members and affiliations.

Kam Movassaghi (Team Co-leader) LA Department of Transportation	Sandra Otto (Team Co-leader) AR Division of FHWA
Jim Brewer KS Department of Transportation	John German Public Works City of San Antonio, TX
Ray Krammes Office of Safety R & D, FHWA	John Okamoto WA Department of Transportation
Wendell Ruff MS Department of Transportation	Seppo Sillan Office of Program Administration, FHWA
Nikiforos Stamatiadis (Report Facilitator) University of Kentucky	Robert Walters AR Department of Transportation

Amplifying Questions

To provide the European hosts with an understanding of the objectives of the scan tour, the team developed a set of amplifying questions that focused on six major topics: project development, design and operating speeds, design solutions for high-volume rural roads, roundabouts, speed moderating techniques on rural roads, and accommodation of bicyclists and pedestrians. These questions were intended to clarify and expand on the team's topics of interest. The questions were grouped on the basis of major concepts within each of the six areas. The amplifying questions developed by the team are listed in Appendix B.

Trip Itinerary

The team toured the five countries from June 3, 2000, through June 18, 2000, as shown below (Table 2). The names of the European contacts for each country are listed in Appendix C. The team also met three times during this period to plan the trip actions and address areas of emphasis (June 3), to review findings and adjust focus if deemed necessary (June 11), and to identify key findings and develop a preliminary list of the team's recommendations (June 17).

Table 2. Scan program dates.

Country	Dates
Sweden	June 4, 2000
Denmark	June 5-6, 2000
The Netherlands	June 8-9, 2000
England	June 12-13, 2000
Germany	June 14-16, 2000

4

Chapter 2
HIGHWAY ADMINISTRATIVE STRUCTURE

This section of the report briefly describes the structure of the highway authority for each country visited. This step established the state of practice of each country regarding roadway geometric design and CSD. The countries are presented in the order in which they were visited.

SWEDEN

The Swedish National Road Administration (SNRA) is the highway agency responsible for planning, designing, constructing, and maintaining the transportation network in Sweden. The country is divided into seven regions, similar to states, and has a roadway network of approximately 421,000 km.[2] A small percentage of these roads (88,000 km) is under the direct responsibility of SNRA and the remaining roads are either municipal (39,000 km) or private roads (284,000 km). However, the bulk of travel (70 percent of vehicle-km) is completed on the state-maintained roads. The SARA has a primary goal "to ensure a socio-economically efficient transport system that is sustainable in the long term for individuals and industry throughout the country." To achieve this goal, five subgoals have been identified, including high accessibility of the system, high transport quality, no fatalities or serious injuries, a good fit in the environment, and promotion of regional development. The most important subgoal among these is the desire to eliminate fatalities and serious injuries (zero mission) by 2007, which is a parliamentary objective regarding road safety.[3]

A strategic infrastructure plan addresses transportation system needs in a 10-year process with a 4-year planning cycle. These plans cover national road and rail requirements and are developed by SNRA in cooperation with regional authorities. Regional plans are developed by regional authorities for each county. The plans include investment schemes, maintenance requirements, safety and environmental concerns, and capacity requirements. The 10-year budget for the national road plan is approximately 87 billion SEK (US$10 billion) with 56 billion SEK allotted to roadway maintenance, which includes operational and rehabilitation costs. To address the zero mission, projects have been reoriented to increase the number and, thus, funding for projects that contribute to the overall safety goal. Funding is also provided by the European Union (EU) for the Trans European Road Network, a roadway network that is similar to the U.S. Interstate system.

DENMARK

The Road Directorate is the state agency of the Ministry of Transport responsible for roadways in Denmark. The Directorate has two primary tasks: 1) road sector activities, including roadway guidelines, research and development, educational responsibilities, maintenance of databases, support and development of policy, and international activities; and 2) highway authority activities, including planning, construction, and operation of the state road network. The Danish roadway network consists of approximately 72,000 km, only 1,650 km of which are under the direct supervision of the Directorate. Approximately 10,000 km are regional roads under the supervision of county agencies, and the remaining local roadways are under the supervision of municipalities. An interesting statistic for Denmark is the average car and bicycle ownership per household: 0.7 cars and 2 bicycles. These vehicle figures also shape the focus of the Road Directorate, which has to address the needs of many more bicyclists while considering vehicle requirements.

In 1993, the Danish Masterplan for Transport was developed with goals to create a new balance by sustaining development in transport, reducing traffic growth, improving alternatives to cars, increasing traffic safety, enhancing the urban environment, and increasing research and development.[4] Specific targets for each of these goals were initially set, such as reducing traffic casualties by 45 percent for the 1988-2000 period, stabilizing CO_2 levels by 2005 to 1988 levels and reducing them by 25 percent by 2030, promoting urban cycling and walking, and improving the traffic environment in urban areas to achieve an overall better quality of life. An additional focal point of this plan is the National Road Safety Policy, which states that "every accident is one too many." This vision guides most of the Danish design approach, which aims to not only achieve the goal stated above but exceed it, if possible. To reduce crashes, safety strategies are focusing on safety of cyclists, speed management, reduced alcohol use and driving, and intersection areas. The focus is on these areas in light of an analysis of crash data that showed approximately 85 percent of all crashes involve at least one of these factors.[5]

> An additional focal point of the Danish plan is the National Road Safety Policy, which states that "every accident is one too many."

The Road Directorate has established a National Cycling Policy to address the needs of the large number of cyclists. The main goal of the policy is not to abandon travel by car but to strengthen travel by bike and increase its use as a transport mode. The main objective of the policy is to improve the urban environment by developing coherent planning and design of a bicycle network, improving maintenance and comfort of bicycle facilities, improving safety, initiating local activities, increasing research, and improving cooperation between state and local authorities. The planning and design philosophy of the Road Directorate for urban areas considers the ease of car travel secondary to traffic safety, the ease of vulnerable users to travel, and public transport.

THE NETHERLANDS

The Ministry of Transport and Public Works is responsible for policy, operation, and research of the Dutch transport network. Five directorates each deal with a specific component of the system, including public works and water management, freight transport, passenger transport, civil aviation, and telecommunications and post. Research centers are part of these directorates, and the Transport Research Center (AVV) is one of three centers with responsibilities for research on infrastructure, statistics, and policy development. The Ministry is responsible for 2,500 km of roadways, which are mostly motorways (freeways), while the remaining 125,000 km are under the responsibility of the local governments.

The Dutch version of safety goals and targets is similar to that of the Swedish and Danish governments. The objective of the plan, called "Sustainable Safety," is to achieve a 50 percent reduction in crashes and a 40 percent reduction in serious injury crashes by 2010.[6] These goals are expected to be achieved by focusing on reduced alcohol use, increased use of seat belts, speed management, separation of cyclists and vehicles, improving hazardous locations, addressing issues regarding heavy vehicles, and providing a road network infrastructure that is self-explaining. Three cardinal rules for sustainable safety include recognizing human limits within the roadway design, developing vehicles that prevent users from getting harmed, and educating users in road behavior. The design approach reflects these objectives as "functionality" (use of roadway as intended), "homogeneity" (no high-speed variations), and "predictability" (roadways should drive as they look). The ultimate objective is development of a uniform roadway network where similar roadways will look and drive alike.

Dutch officials are currently reviewing geometric design guidelines and reclassifying roadways to conform with their new classification concept.

The Dutch Ministry is taking several steps to reach its goal of sustainable safety, including introducing uniform speed limits in residential areas of 30 km/h in urban and 60 km/h in rural areas, altering the priority rules in roundabouts, increasing public education campaigns, and incorporating safety audits as part of a uniform design check. Phase 1 of the sustainable safety program will cost approximately 400 million guilders (US$200 million), half of which will come from the central government and half from the provincial and local governments. Implementation of the next phase requires an investment of 12 billion guilders (US$6 billion); the entire program will cost approximately 30 billion (US$15 billion). Currently, 60 percent of the urban and 40 percent of the rural roadway network have been converted to enforce the concept of the new lower speeds. Several other roadways are also in the process of conversion. Finally, an underlying precept in all these plans is the commitment to "making better use of the existing system," which demonstrates the decision to utilize existing resources to their fullest capacity.

> Projects are categorized based on their impact on safety, environment, economy, accessibility, and integration within the existing system.

ENGLAND

The Highways Agency is the responsible authority for maintaining, operating, and improving the 6,500 miles of trunk roads and motorways in England. The government has charged the Highways Agency to maintain, operate, and improve the motorway and trunk road network in support of the government's transport and land-use planning policies.[7] Several objectives will help meet this goal, including reducing congestion, minimizing the roadway impact to the natural and built environment, improving safety for all road users, promoting choice and information for travelers, and shifting the focus to maintenance of roadways instead of new construction. This shift in focus necessitates a more efficient use of existing roadways and development of a prioritized list of improvements. Projects are categorized based on their impact on safety, environment, economy, accessibility, and integration within the existing system.

As in the other countries, a road safety strategy targets a 40 percent reduction in fatalities and serious injuries by 2010 accompanied by a 10 percent reduction in slight injuries for all non-motorways and trunk roads in Great Britain.[8] Target groups including vehicle occupants, bicyclists, high-risk age groups, heavy vehicles, and roadway workers have been identified as potential means for reaching these figures. Several initiatives are under way for each of these target groups. For example, road layouts that encourage safer driver behavior have been introduced to address car occupant issues; more initiatives have been taken to reduce drinking and driving; higher emphasis has been placed on developing the National Cycle Network and supporting implementation of safer bicycle routes; and research is under way to identify problems of teenage and elderly drivers.

The Agency also has taken a new role in operating the network to make better use of existing roadways through the use of technological developments and innovative ideas. Promoting use of public transport and making bicycle lanes more attractive are two of the schemes that the Agency employs in improving service without building new roads. To further promote these schemes, the Agency developed a tool kit that provides techniques and innovative ideas for managing, maintaining, and developing roadways. Furthermore, the Agency has recently developed a new Environmental Strategic Plan that ensures controlled and reduced impact of roadways on the environment.[9]

GERMANY

The agency responsible for roadway planning, design, and construction is the Division for Roads and Road Transport, which is part of the Federal Ministry of Transport, Building, and Housing. This Division has several subdivisions with varied responsibilities, including environmental protection, research, road traffic engineering, acquisition of right of way, and development of federal transport networks for the various states, known as "laender." Three road categories, including federal state roads and municipal roads, are classified as federal highways and thus are under the supervision of the Division. Each state is responsible for constructing, maintaining, and operating the federal roads on behalf of the Federal Ministry and is invited to use relevant guidelines for planning, designing, constructing, and maintaining the state roads.

The design guidelines used in the past have been recently evaluated and modified to address design consistency. The new guidelines are simply recommended practices for all roads, except federal highways, which require a more strict approach to the guidelines. Due, in part, to financial constraints, these new guidelines were developed under the notion that only necessary roads are to be built, not ideal or wider roads. This approach was based on the idea that roads should be built to a more human scale and minimize environmental impact issues.

SUMMARY

All countries visited share some common characteristics with respect to their highway agencies. One national agency is responsible for developing and maintaining the national motorway system, which typically is a small fraction of the entire roadway network. Each government has given these agencies a safety mandate, with target levels ranging from no fatalities to a 40 percent reduction in fatalities and serious injuries. This focus on safety sets the stage for most actions regarding roadway geometric design and project development that address targeted groups of roadway users.

Chapter 3
SCAN RESULTS

The U.S. delegation met with numerous representatives from transportation and highway ministries, research organizations, and consultants who shared many interesting ideas and insights on the scan tour topics. This chapter presents practices the delegation found most significant and those that may be beneficial for the U.S. environment. Additionally, it identifies and discusses practices that may be transferable to the U.S. context.

PROJECT PLANNING

The countries visited all have an underlying philosophy of a project planning process aiming to improve safety while remaining sensitive to the needs of the community. As noted in the previous section, all agencies are responding to a safety mandate, which affects their project development process through a focus on improving the existing system by making better use of it. The following three steps are typically followed in the project development process. First, a project need is identified either on the basis of long-term plans or through a political request. Second, a feasibility study is performed to determine and examine alternatives and seek public input. Third, a final design is developed for the project construction and completion. This process typically covers a 10-year period with periodic updates.

Although this general approach is followed in all countries visited, some differences exist with regard to how this general plan is applied. For example, SNRA has a set of guiding maxims to follow during the project development. These maxims include quality assurance, community planning, transparency (open mindedness and decisions involving the public), environmental concerns, safety, clearly explained decisions, and assurance of public understanding of these decisions. In Denmark, after the completion of certain stages of the process, parliamentary support is required to continue with the project. At the end of the initial project concept, an Act of Design is required in which the need for the project is demonstrated and authorization to continue is granted. After completion of the preliminary design, an Act of Construction is sought to support development of the final design. After a final design has been selected, a funding request is submitted to the Parliament and the project is included in the national budget. In the Netherlands, one of the initial steps includes definition of the relationship of the proposed project to existing government policies and a request for political support by all levels of government. Moreover, after the completion of the preliminary design a statement by the Minister of Transport is required that identifies proposed alternatives and documents the project's importance and significance. This project planning process is described in one of the Dutch laws (Tracè Law), and the final design of the project becomes a Tracè law. The Highways Agency in England also has recently developed a process by which all proposed projects on a route are evaluated in light of a Route Management Strategy that has been prepared for that route. The route and project evaluations are based on the following five criteria: safety, economy, environment, system integration, and network accessibility. Moreover, studies are completed that consider other modes of transport in conjunction with roadway projects to determine whether other travel modes can accommodate the travel needs more efficiently. So far, this new approach has been applied to three routes, and the Agency is satisfied with the results of the process. Germany has somewhat different stages for urban and inter-urban projects. For urban areas, decisions are made on the basis of four themes that consider traffic volumes, environmental concerns, town planning and road space issues, and economics. For federal inter-urban projects, the requirements are defined by law, which is preceded by a formal procedure where the choice is evaluated on the basis of a microeconomic analysis.

Generally, the project development process in the countries visited is similar to that of the United States; however, differences were noted. A major difference is that in Europe a longer period of time is devoted to the planning process and longer sections, typically entire corridors, are considered. Such an approach provides the opportunity for long-range planning by allowing for a more systematic overview and for defining needs and deficiencies over the entire system. Another difference in the process is greater European emphasis in urban areas on integrating projects in communities by addressing the public's concerns for speed management and aesthetics. Integrating both human and natural environmental concerns is an integral part of their project development process. An example is shown in Figures 1 and 2, where a park was placed over a freeway section to address noise and visual pollution in Germany.

Figure 1 Freeway lid with park, Germany.

Figure 2 Park view of the freeway lid, Germany.

The delegation was also impressed by the level and impact of public involvement. All five countries involve the public in their project development process, although degrees and levels of involvement varied by project type and country. Sweden has legislative requirements for public involvement and SNRA solicits public input even in projects for which it is not legally required because Swedish officials believe it is good public policy and can provide them with additional support in later stages of the project. Local communities have the final decision on projects that pass through their communities, but they have less say in projects in rural areas. In Denmark, stakeholders of a project are involved in various stages of the project development, and the public is involved either passively through information dissemination or actively through consultation or participation in the design process. The Netherlands has recently implemented a new approach for public involvement. This approach is based on design workshops in which all alternatives for a project are worked out simultaneously by a group of experts and stakeholders. All of these alternatives are then presented at a public meeting, where the public's assistance is sought to define the best alternative. This approach has been applied in some projects, and the Dutch believe that the process was successful. In England, the public is informed through press announcements, and specific stakeholders are involved at various stages. Route seminars are held for invited stakeholders to discuss project objectives and to identify potential problem areas and possible solutions. Value management workshops are presented to a smaller group of stakeholders to identify specific actions to be taken to determine the final design choice. Finally, the public can comment on the final choice; however, the Agency has the final say. Germany permits a higher public involvement for urban projects, since such projects have a more direct impact on individuals. Public meetings and work groups are an integral part of project development: consensus is sought and the old concept of simply announcing the project to the public has been abandoned. For inter-urban projects, the public can appeal the final design and alignment of the project, but there are time limits on comments and appeals.

Some of these concepts and methods to involve the public in project development are potentially transferable to the United States and could prove beneficial in streamlining existing practices. The use of the Dutch design workshops, in which alternatives developed by experts and stakeholders are presented to the public to select the best alternative, is a method that deserves additional exploration. Moreover, involvement of the public at the earliest stage possible was stressed by all governments to avoid potential conflicts and problems after the project has

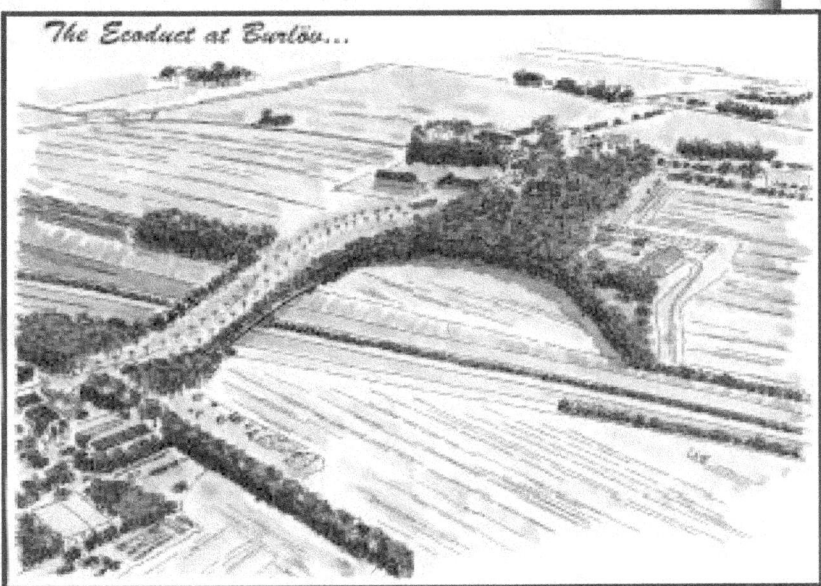

The Ecoduct at Burlöv...

Figure 3. Artistic rendering of bridge overpass with plants, Sweden.

been fully developed. The use of artistic renderings as visual aids to graphically show the finished project is very important in gaining public acceptance and understanding (Figure 3). Distribution at public meetings of detailed pamphlets that identify the affected area and the rationale for selecting the proposed options can enhance and improve the public's understanding of the project (Figure 4). Some additional observations include the use of safety audits as an evaluation tool for overall project design, the development of project budgets at the end of the process, and the greater role of state and local politics in the project development process. The scan team concluded that no single approach can solve all potential problems in project development, and a reasonable mix of practices is essential.

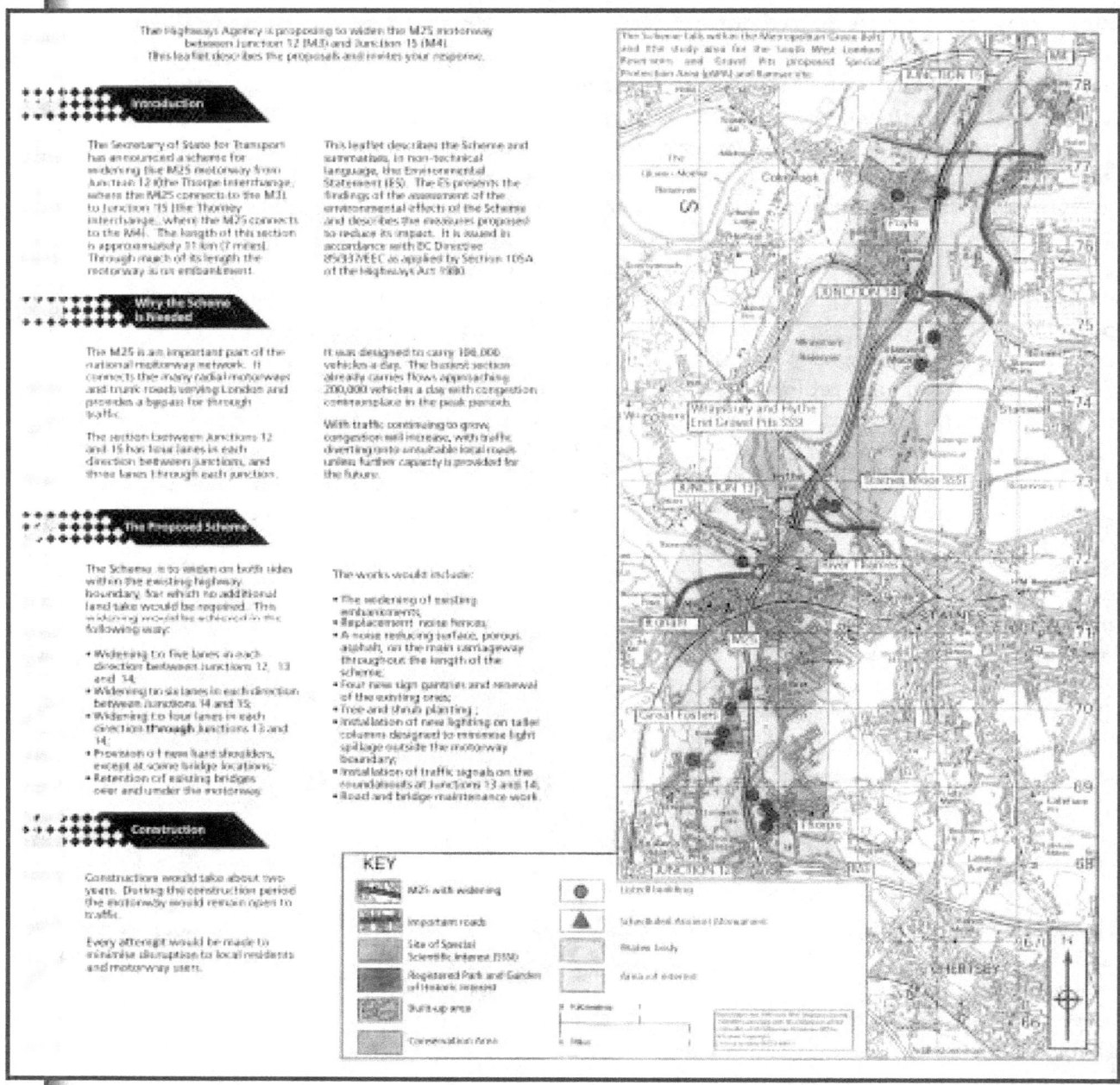

Figure 4. Pamphlet inviting public involvement, England.

ENVIRONMENTAL CONSIDERATIONS

All the countries visited include environmental issues as an integral part of the project. It was interesting to find that several countries have copied or adapted the U.S. National Environmental Policy Act (NEPA) process but they have integrated it more efficiently within the project development process. The Dutch believe that recognition of environmental concerns is an everyday practice and that those concerns are addressed sufficiently through their normal design process. Currently, Dutch officials are considering means by which the regulations and process can be streamlined to reduce project completion time. The English use a design manual to guide environmental impact analysis (EIA) and environmental design in which a proper and full examination of all environmental considerations relevant to the project are presented. They have also recently initiated a new approach to appraisal (NATA) in which all impacts of a project are defined within five overall objectives (environment, safety, economy, accessibility, and integration) either quantitatively or qualitatively. It is expected that application of the NATA as a high-level tool for appraising projects will help to address environmental factors in making initial investment decisions.

One general observation was that the highway agencies of these countries are very committed to addressing environmental issues. Most of the issues presented appeared to be human related, including noise and historical preservation concerns. The reliance on local governmental agencies to develop environmental impact studies (EIS) was also presented as an alternative to identifying problems and possible solutions more easily and at the local level. For ease of project development and faster completion, projects are often restricted to within the existing right of way. The concept of land redistribution was also presented as a method of mitigation. A simple example of this approach is shown in Figure 5, where the new road will bisect both land parcels. To avoid access problems and maintain continuous property for each land owner, the land parcels 1 and 2 cut by the road are swapped between the two owners. This practice seems to address some accessibility issues and merits further review for application in the United States. Finally, European Union (EU) laws and directives regarding environmental issues play an important role and are addressed in the project development process.

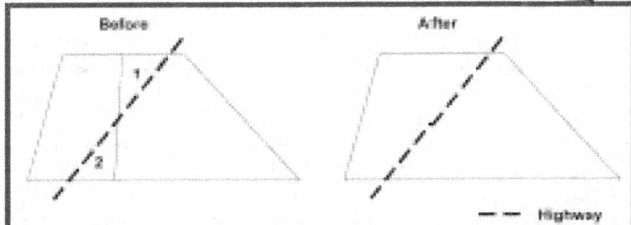

Figure 5. Land redistribution concept.

SPEEDS

Even though each country used a different term to describe their design speed, all use a guiding speed for designing roadways that ties the various roadway elements. In Sweden, the term "reference speed" is used to denote the existing or planned speed limit of the road. For new rural roads, a speed of 70, 90, or 110 km/h is selected based on the road type. Under this scheme, motorways and semi-motorways (two-lane, two-way roads with full access control) use a speed of 110 km/h, while the choice between 90 or 70 km/h is made based on the geometrics of the road. A new concept that has been applied only in urban areas so far is the "environmental reference speed," which is a speed used in designing roadways in such a way that it is difficult to drive above this speed. In Denmark, a desired speed is defined, which represents the upper limit of the driver's comfort level. To address safety, a design speed is used that is equal to the desired speed plus 20 km/h and also reflects actual operating speed for inter-urban roads. The relation between desired speeds and roadway categories for urban roads is shown in Table 8.[19] Until recently, design speeds in the Netherlands were 120 km/h for roads with right shoulders and heavy vehicles, 100 km/h for motorways, 80-90 km/h for roads with either no right shoulder or heavy vehicles (or rural, un-divided roads), 60-70 km/h for roads with no right shoulder (urban arterials), 50 km/h for arterials, and 30 km/h for residential access roads. In the future, only three road categories will exist, and then the design speeds will be 120 km/h for urban and rural freeways, 50-80 km/h for urban and rural distributors, and 30-60 km/h for urban and rural access roads.

Table 3. Speeds and categories of urban roadways in Denmark.[10]

Traffic intensity	Roadway function				
	A	B	C	D	E
I	120-90	_¹	_²	NA	NA
II	100-80	80-70	_¹	_²	NA
III	80-60	70-60	30-50	_¹	_²
IV	70-60	60-50	40-50	20-30	_¹
V		_³	_³	none	none
VI		_³	_³	_³	none

Notes: NA, not applicable; ¹ problematic combination; ² extra problematic combination; ³ not currently recommended

The design speed in Germany is determined on the basis of the roadway to be designed.[11] A matrix is used that identifies possible combinations between traffic intensity and roadway function (Table 4). Categories A, B, and C provide connection between urban centers, while category D provides higher access to local areas, and category E is mainly for direct access (and thus, no design speeds are used). There is a hierarchy among urban centers that defines what type of connection is to be provided. The entire German roadway network is based on the concept that certain minimum travel times need to be achieved: 60, 30, and 15 minutes of travel time between urban centers and villages. These rules also shape the roadway category and, thus, the choice of the design speed. The design speed choice is made by the road planning group, which could be the local or regional planning agencies. The design speed of the roadway is a design aspect that is determined by the planning team, and the public cannot influence its selection. The design team typically selects the design speed on the basis of issues that need to be addressed and the goals to be achieved. The choice is usually based on a combination of cost considerations, safety concerns, and environmental issues.

Table 4. Roadway categories and design speed in Germany.

Roadway type	Traffic intensity/ speed (km/h)			
	Very low 10-20	Low 30-40	Medium 50	High 60-70
Traffic roads (through traffic and traffic between urban centers)		✓	✓	✓
Local roads	✓	✓	(✓)¹	

Note: ¹ possible but not desirable

Finally, in England a range of speeds for each roadway category exists that is more narrow than the ranges suggested in the Green Book. The parameters that control this choice are alignment constraint, which describes frequency of curves; layout constraint, which describes access frequency and roadway cross section; and mandatory speed limits. The design speed for rural roads is defined using the diagram in Figure 6, where for urban roads the design speed is approximately 5 km/h higher than the speed limit.[25]

A roadway design philosophy common to all countries was the reliance on the physical roadway design to "enforce" operating speeds. This philosophy could be considered as a speed management approach in which the objective is not simply to reduce speed but to provide a roadway planned and designed in such a way that an appropriate speed is obtained, thus, a "consistent" or "self-explaining" look for each road category can be achieved. This is the concept of the self-explaining, self-enforcing road, in which roads are designed for a specific purpose or function (Figure 7). The Europeans address safety in an efficient way for all users by implementing an aesthetic approach to explain the road function and enforce speeds. This approach also allows them to establish speed limits close to the expected operating speeds and thus avoid higher travel speeds. An interesting observation was the lack of speed enforcement by the police and the greater emphasis placed on other enforcement means, such as roadway geometry or automatic cameras. It should be noted, however, that reliance on roadway geometry to enforce speeds was more prominent in urban settings. Moreover, all countries have set national speed limits for each road category and area type (urban or rural).

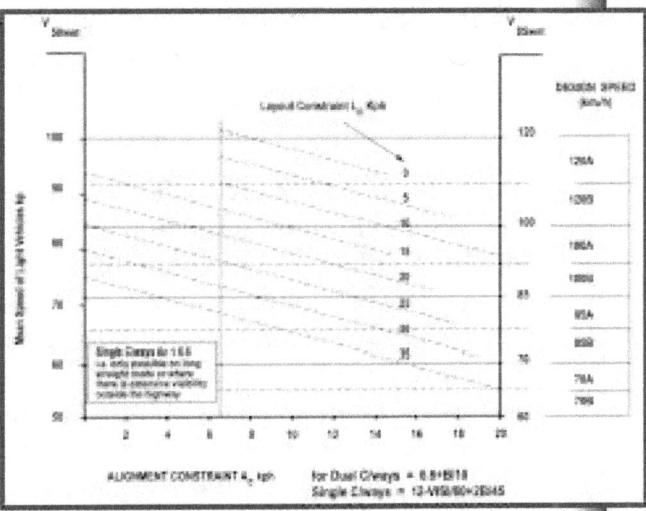

Figure 6. Design speed nomograph, England.[25]

Figure 7. Self-enforcing, self-explaining road, The Netherlands.

Another observation was the acceptance of lower operating speeds by the road users in these countries compared with the levels of acceptance in the United States. This attitude may reflect the design approach of a self-enforcing roadway design and higher public acceptance of such roads.

DESIGN FLEXIBILITY

All countries visited utilize design guidelines for roadway design that are considered central to their design philosophy. These guidelines are typically more strict for motorways and are applied more as standards and with greater conformity to these roads. All countries visited have a design exception process through which to address departures from design guidelines. This process is more frequently applied to non-motorways. It was also noted that, in general, the public more easily accepts the lack of flexibility in motorway design because of the purpose of these roads —mobility is gained at the expense of aesthetic treatment. Greater design flexibility was observed for urban and rural non-motorways that typically are responsive to site-specific limitations. Thus, the wider acceptability of such design departures may be due to the fact that each problem area is addressed within its context and constraints.

Commitment to creating a roadway environment that addresses safety, capacity, economic, and environmental concerns has also shaped the wider acceptance of design flexibility. The British Design Manual has a section for such deviations in each roadway component that discusses possible reasons for deviating (relaxing) the suggested guidelines.[12] This approach reinforces the concept of adjusting the roadway design to the specific local requirements. It should be noted that although the Manual emphasizes the use of appropriate design and implementation of desirable values, at the same time it arms the designer with possible flexibility.

All these countries have or are currently revising their design guidelines. This process may have made them more aware of the need to view their design guidelines as a flexible tool for those designs where human and environmental needs may play a stronger role in shaping the final roadway design. In addition, realizing the possible limitations of the previous guidelines may have significantly impacted current acceptance of such flexibility, since the new guidelines are now geared to address road purpose and to create a uniform look for each road category. The experience of developing new guidelines has allowed these agencies to understand the value of design flexibility and exceptions.

Set documentation, which was very extensive in England, is required to justify departures from the design guidelines. Morever, the Highways Agency in England has a manual that describes how and when design departures are to be requested and identifies the types of documentation needed to support such a request.[13] In a typical project, the designer has to visualize the project and determine how to approach it. Then, each departure needs to be justified and explained to the Safety Office of the Agency, which has ultimate decision authority. Several components of the project are set, similar to the AASHTO minimum criteria, and these components require official documentation. Designers have the latitude to alter other, more minor components at their discretion to address the specific needs of the project. In general, the countries are shielded from legal liability regarding design defects. The exception is England where litigation is expanding regarding departure from design guidelines; most of the litigation is settled out of court.

In the countries visited, the guidelines issued by the national highway authorities are usually considered as recommendations for any projects under the authority of local governmental agencies. This provides great flexibility in designing to meet the local needs and conditions.

RURAL ROADS

High speeds on rural roads are also a safety issue for those countries, which experience a high number of runoff crashes. In Sweden for example, runoff crashes on two-lane roads comprise a third of all crashes on these roads (115 of a total of 339). Moreover, almost all of the runoff crashes occur on two-lane roads (100 of a total 115). Similar percentages were also noted for other countries as well. Head on crashes were the second most common type of crash in most of these countries. A typical cross section of rural roads in some countries is 13 m, with 5.5-m travel lanes and 1.0-m shoulders (Sweden and Denmark) while in England a 9.3-m cross section is used, with 3.65-m travel lanes and 1.0-m shoulders (i.e., 7.3-m carriageway plus 2 x 1.0-m hardstrips). In Germany a 10.5-m cross section is used, with 3.75-m travel lanes and 1.5-m shoulders. To address capacity issues, wider cross sections are used in England, with 5-m travel lanes, which also allows better overtaking for improved flow and is also safer than the standard width. However, the Swedes have indicated that these wider roads have not had a good safety record.

The major contributing factor to the high number of runoff crashes is high speeds, so those countries are focusing on attempts to control and reduce speeds. To achieve this objective, higher speeds are eliminated to preserve safety. This is manifested in the lower design speeds and speed limits for rural roads as well as in efforts to implement the self-explaining, self-enforcing concept on these roadways.

With the exception of the Netherlands, all countries visited use a common treatment on high-volume rural roadways, namely the conversion of a two-lane roadway to a 2+1 facility in lieu of four-lane facilities (Figure 8). On such roads the third (middle) lane serves as a passing lane in which the right of way alternates periodically. Each country has customized this design to conform to its design guidelines and safety goals, including use of varied roadway widths, lengths of passing lanes, median cable guardrail, and end treatment of passing lanes. For example, in England and Sweden these roads have been retrofitted (within the same right of way) to wider cross sections of 12 m and 13 m, respectively. The passing lane has a width of 3.5 m and the remaining travel width is evenly split between the other two lanes. In Germany a slightly wider right of way is used and a 15.5-m cross section is utilized (Figure 9). In Sweden a cable barrier is used to separate the two directions of travel, and the safety experience

Figure 8. Example of 2+1 road, Germany.

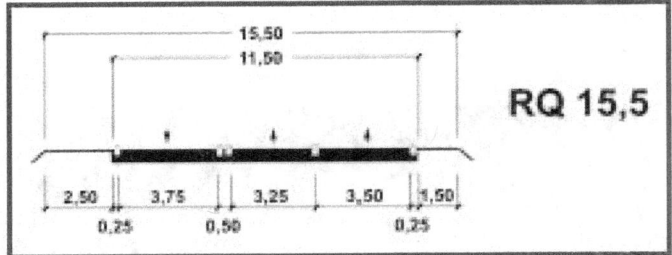

Figure 9. Cross section for German 2+1 roads.

Figure 10. Use of cable barrier in 2+1 road, Sweden.

Figure 11. 2+1 road without median separator, Denmark.

Figure 12. Narrow lane widths, The Netherlands.

Figure 13. Optical narrowing by eliminating centerline, Sweden.

with these roadways has been good (Figures 10 and 11). The Germans, on the other hand, do not favor the use of cable barriers because of safety concerns. The German experience indicates that these roadways can have similar capacities as four-lane divided roads without shoulders, and when four-lane roads present safety problems they are converted to 2+1 facilities. Finally, all countries that use this design indicated that to facilitate conversion and reduce costs, they utilize the existing right of way.

Overall, all agencies indicated capacity gains and safety improvements from the use of this design, which may be transferable to the United States. This practice is similar to the U.S. passing lanes on two-lane roads, but it would be done for longer roadway sections. It should be pointed out that additional research may be required to evaluate the use of these roadways in the United States, particularly since some countries indicated that they are experiencing higher speeds and more crashes around the merging area (Germany).

Another approach for improving safety on these roads is the use of narrower lane widths, which requires drivers to slow down. This approach is implemented either by physically creating narrower travelways (Figure 12) or by visually decreasing the available width. The more widely used techniques in optically narrowing the road are painting wider edge lines or eliminating centerline striping (Figure 13). It should be noted that this optical narrowing is a concept more often used for low-volume, rural roads. To further enforce the narrower roadway concept, clear zones are typically not provided in some countries (Sweden and Denmark), and some roadway objects are shielded by guardrails. These measures are applied to non-motorways where flexibility exists in design guidelines, rather than to motorways for which the guidelines are more rigid.

TRAFFIC CALMING

A strong commitment to reducing speeds through urban areas was a common concept among all countries visited. The Danish Road Directorate has developed a guide that describes possible means for reducing speeds through urban areas with specific design elements.[14] A European Community project is also under way, called Developing Urban Management and Safety (DUMAS), which is examining speed management in urban areas in Denmark, the Netherlands, and England. The practices of each of these countries are summarized in a report by the Danish Road Directorate,[15] and additional guidelines for evaluating speed management techniques in urban areas were recently published.[16] Finally, the Department of the Environment in the United Kingdom has developed a series of leaflets that summarize concepts, principles, and examples of traffic calming devices.[17]

Numerous practices have been implemented in urban areas to reduce speeds:

> Prewarnings: typically lines on the pavement with (rumble strips) or without punishment (lines and traffic signs);

> Gates: typically different pavement color or structures that indicate transition between traffic environments, often augmented with signs and landscaping (Figures 14 and 15);

> Narrowings: typically the available travelway width is reduced to narrower lane widths with the addition of islands, by eliminating one lane in two-lane roads or by using wider edge markings (Figures 18-19);

> Humps and tables: with varied profiles including circular, sinusoidal, dome-shaped, or trapezoidal cross-sections and

Figure 14. Example of gate, Germany.

Figure 15. Example of gate with a platform, Sweden.

Figure 16. Landscaping to narrow lane width, Germany.

Figure 17. Narrowing with humps, Denmark.

Figure 18. Narrowing with signs, Denmark.

Figure 19. Narrowing by eliminating one lane, The Netherlands.

Figure 20. Speed hump, England.

Figure 21. Combination of several traffic calming elements: islands, roundabout, and narrow lanes, Denmark.

varied lengths depending upon the desired speed reduction (Figure 20);

Raised areas: typically a trapezoidal hump with extended length to allow for longer vehicles to have all wheels on them;

Staggering: typically a lane is shifted over;

Roundabouts: typically used as gates for speed reduction (Figures 21 and 22);

Chicanes: typically extensions of the curb at intersections to reduce approach lane widths;

Islands: typically raised elements along the centerline of the roadway to shelter pedestrians and ease street crossing (Figure 23);

Cushions: typically square humps in each travel lane (Figure 24);

Landscaping and plantings: typically use of vegetation as gates, as a means to visually reduce lane widths or as methods to enforce other traffic calming components; and

Pavement textures and colors: typically use of stones or pavers to visually separate roadway elements, and use of colors to enforce concepts or mark transitions between roadway environments (Figures 25-27), (26 and 27 displayed on page 22).

The goal of these devices is primarily to reduce speeds, and they achieve their objective by forcing drivers to drive through them at lower speeds.[124] In all countries visited the use of these devices produced the desired speed reductions, which ranged from a few km/h to 20 km/h.[125] Safety gains also materialized from the use of traffic calming schemes, and crash numbers were reduced —in some cases by more than 60 percent (Denmark and England). It should be mentioned here that the most effective traffic calming means are humps, but they require precision in design and construction to achieve a comfortable ride when traversed at the desired speed.[129]

For successful implementation, an area-wide strategy is required with a systemic rather than a localized solution. This reinforces the concept of traffic calming for the entire area by giving the driver a clear and continuous message. Because of the likelihood that not all components of the plan will be constructed at the same time, an area-wide strategy ensures that all individual components will be part of the total solution. An additional element for successful implementation is use of consistent or similar treatment elements throughout the area. Such consistency avoids continually surprising drivers with new designs, which results in inappropriate behavior.

An additional goal of the highway agencies in the countries visited is integration of all modes and users in the same space in urban centers. Several of the traffic calming elements presented here are utilized to achieve this objective. For example, raised areas are used to indicate pedestrian crossings and alert motorists of the presence of other users; different pavement colors are used to indicate bikeways sharing the same travelway with vehicles; and narrowings are used to provide parking spaces and pedestrian access.

Another important aspect is the requirement that each traffic calming element be properly designed for the intended travel speed. This will result in a roadway uncomfortable to drivers exceeding the speed but not to those who travel at the desired speed. This design aspect is especially important for humps, bumps, cushions, and raised areas, since all create vertical rises and may cause discomfort. Finally, community acceptance is also very important for successful implementation.

Several communities throughout the United States have utilized various traffic calming elements. Most of the elements presented in this report are transferable to the U.S. urban

Figure 22. Small roundabout flush with pavement, Sweden.

Figure 23. Combination of several traffic calming elements: islands, narrow lanes, and pavement textures, Denmark.

Figure 24. Cushions, England.

Figure 25. Lane markings as part of pavement texture, Denmark.

Figure 26. Chicane and pavement texture, Germany.

Figure 27. Table with different pavement texture, Denmark.

environment. However, differences in land use, development, and transportation users between Europe and the United States must be recognized. For example, the automobile-dominated society and urban structure in the United States is in stark contrast to the extensive use of public and other modes of transportation in European cities. Moreover, the goal of improving safety is considered more important than mobility by European highway agencies and, thus, the use of these traffic calming schemes is accepted more easily by the European public.

ROUNDABOUTS

Roundabouts are used extensively in all countries visited and are considered an effective form of traffic control at intersections. Four of the five countries each have more than 1,000 roundabouts (Sweden has approximately 900), with the Netherlands having approximately 2,000 in existence. Each country has developed design guidelines to address the specific geometric design aspects.[30-34] Two general philosophies guide the design components of roundabouts. The first concept is that the flared, tangential approach provides for a smoother path for vehicles, where the aesthetic component of the roundabout is overlooked in favor of creating a path around the circle that allows comfortable travel without significant loss of speed. This approach is used to enhance capacity and allow higher entry speeds. The second concept is the radial approach, where lower entry speeds force drivers to slow down when entering the intersection. The latter roundabouts are used more as speed reduction and traffic calming devices. The first design concept is used in England and Sweden, while the second design concept is used in the other three countries.

Irrespective of the design philosophy, roundabouts are considered a very safe form of intersection in all five countries. Various levels of safety gains have been achieved with the installation of roundabouts, but the overall trends are positive. For example, a Danish study of 201 roundabouts showed a 71 percent reduction in injury crashes after the installation of roundabouts, while a Swedish study of 21 urban intersections showed a 85 percent reduction in injury crashes after the installation.[35] A similar study of 200 sites in the Netherlands indicated a 51 percent reduction in all crashes and a 72 percent reduction in casualty crashes. As these safety studies indicate, significant reductions in fatality and injury crashes materialized after the installation of roundabouts. A few issues, however, should be pointed out here. First, despite significant reductions in the severity of crashes, the reduction in the overall number of crashes is sometimes not as large. Second, most of these sites were not signalized intersections and, thus, the safety gains at signalized intersections may be lower, since there is the likelihood of higher safety concerns at such intersections. Third, there may be significant differences in the level of safety gains between urban and rural areas because of the differences in travel speeds. Finally, significant differences in safety gains are realized by various types of road users, with passenger car users having the highest gains and pedestrians and bicyclists having the lowest. Overall, however, these empirical data that demonstrate the safety improvement from roundabouts can be used in the United States to supplement and support the early U.S. experience with roundabouts and to support their further usage and implementation.

Roundabouts can also improve intersection capacity over signalization; those with single-lane approaches seem to perform very well, with volumes of up to 2,500 vehicles per hour (Figures 28 and 29). Even though this estimate was provided by all the agencies as a general upper limit rule of thumb for one-lane approaches, roundabouts are also used on roads with significantly higher daily traffic volumes. For example, in the Netherlands they are used on roads with 5,000 to 40,000 vehicles per day. The radial approach entry, i.e., the centerlines of the approaches pass through the center of the inscribed circle, is encouraged to facilitate both sight distance issues and to provide a smooth entry in and exit from the roundabout. However, the safety gains

Figure 28. One-lane rural roundabout with bike lane, The Netherlands.

Figure 29. One-lane urban roundabout, England.

Figure 30. Roundabout with three lanes and traffic signal control, England.

experienced are typically due to reductions in speeds through the roundabout that may reduce mobility and create delays to through traffic. To increase capacity within the roundabout, some countries are implementing multi-lane approaches and signalization (Figure 30), which may affect safety levels. Another means for increasing capacity is the provision of exclusive right-turn lanes or bays at the

Figure 31. Small roundabout, England.

Figure 32. Medium-size roundabout, Denmark.

Figure 33. Exclusive bike path on roundabout, Denmark.

Figure 34. Separated and colored bikeway on roundabout, Denmark.

appropriate roundabout approaches. Roundabouts are particularly successful where the traffic flows are in balance on all approach legs. Roundabouts are a less effective form of intersection when the number of entry legs exceeds four, mainly because of the size of the junction and the higher circulating speeds that can be achieved.

An additional significant observation is that four of the five countries visited (all but England) have, to date, only used single-lane roundabouts and are now starting to consider and introduce double-lane roundabouts. The four countries (Sweden, Denmark, the Netherlands, and Germany) have used roundabouts primarily as a safety tool and a speed reduction measure, whereas England, which has used roundabouts longer, uses them more for operational benefits.

Roundabouts provide the designer with the flexibility to adjust the design to site-specific conditions. An example of this flexibility is the use of tear-drop-shaped roundabouts at interchanges in Sweden. This design eliminates the need for traffic signals or other traffic controls at the interchange, creates a safer environment for left-turning traffic, and improves capacity because of lower levels of delays. The size of the roundabout is also important. It is a flexible design element and each country has adopted different minimum radii for the central island (Figures 31 and 32). For example, in Sweden the minimum radius for the central island to accommodate trucks and buses is 10 m, while in England the minimum is 4 m. The size of the roundabout will also be affected by the design philosophy to either address capacity or reduce speed, which in turn will have an impact on the right-of-way requirements.

One issue of concern is the interaction among vehicles, pedestrians, and bicycles and the best integration of these users within the roundabout. Some countries are separating the travel lanes of vehicles and other users by creating separate paths (Figures 33 and 34). In these designs, vehicles have the right of way and islands are provided for the other users when they are needed for crossing the roadway. In other countries, bicyclists have their own lanes and thus, have the right of way in the roundabout.

BICYCLISTS AND PEDESTRIANS

All countries visited address and consider seriously the needs of bicyclists and pedestrians. Depending on the country's national policy, two different philosophies apply to the level of consideration for these users. Sweden, Denmark, and the Netherlands place a high importance on addressing the needs of these users and often provide separate facilities as part of their network. Moreover, there is a systematic effort in these countries to promote alternative use of transport modes, and thus cycling and walking are heavily promoted. A recently completed project, sponsored by the European Community, identified the best practices to promote cycling and walking.[158] This project identified ways to promote and encourage cycling and provides a list of means to improve existing cycling and pedestrian facilities. The national cycling policy in Denmark, for example, is advocating that there is no need to abandon the automobile, but to strengthen the use of bike and other transport modes (Figure 35). On the other hand, Germany and England consider these users in their planning process but they give

Figure 35. Bike parking facility, Denmark.

them lower priority when compared with the other countries. One reason for this difference may be that levels of demand are lower in Germany and England than in the other countries. For example, in Denmark each household has on average two bikes, in contrast to 0.7 automobiles per household; data from the Netherlands indicate that more than 50 percent of trips are non-motorized.

A national network bicycle plan (in various states of completion) exists for all countries visited. Additional sections are obviously added where needed, but Sweden, Denmark, and the Netherlands consider their networks complete. In most countries the highway agencies are charged with development of the network but the local authorities are mostly responsible for providing the specific plans and final designs. Furthermore, community organizations and non-governmental agencies are cooperating with the highway agencies in several countries to develop guides for such facilities from their perspective. An example of such an effort is a guide developed by the Swedish Association of Local Authorities that presents ideas and concepts regarding use of town streets by both motorized and non-motorized users.[159]

All five countries place an equal importance on the mobility needs of bicyclists and pedestrians in urban areas and frequently give them higher priority than the mobility needs of vehicles. This philosophy is manifested in their efforts to promote

Figure 36. Bike path elevated and separated from roadway, Denmark.

Figure 37. Bike path separated by road markings, Denmark.

Figure 38. Bike lane separated with color coding, Denmark.

Figure 39. Rural bike facility parallel to roadway, The Netherlands.

use of bicycling and walking either by national campaigns (Netherlands and Denmark) or by constructing dedicated facilities for these users as part of improvement projects (England). Additional efforts include using traffic calming devices as part of urban areas, reducing parking spaces in urban centers, and reducing speed limits (to increase travel times while attempting to improve safety). In Denmark, for example, there has been a systematic effort to reduce car parking spaces by 2 to 3 percent to promote cycling and walking.

In most countries separate facilities are provided (Figures 36-42, this page and opposite) and whenever possible pedestrians and bicyclists are also separated to improve safety. Even though significant efforts are made to address pedestrian and bicyclist needs, some cases still exist where their needs are overlooked or not addressed properly. An example of such a problem is the conversion of exclusive facilities to shared use where one of the two groups loses the exclusive use of the pathway. In another case, use of facilities that alternate at intervals from side to side of the vehicle roadway creates additional crossings that require careful design and may be detrimental to safety.

All countries are struggling with integrating pedestrians and cyclists into roundabouts. Denmark and the Netherlands provide completely separate paths for these users (Figures 43 and 44, opposite page) while the other countries provide paths within the same travelway. In most countries, pedestrian safety is good at roundabouts, since the design affords the opportunity to provide crossing facilities on the approaches. However, for bicyclists there are more concerns, since crashes are likely under-reported. To improve these estimates, the Swedish agency has currently started an effort to collect crash data from hospitals in addition to police records.

Figure 40. Urban bike facility parallel to roadway, The Netherlands.

Figure 41. Bike and pedestrian paths separated by color, Germany.

Figure 43. Bike path and roundabout crossing on separate paths, The Netherlands.

Figure 42. Shared pedestrian path and bicycle facility, Germany.

Figure 44. Bike path sharing the roadway, but color coded, Denmark.

Chapter Four
RECOMMENDATIONS AND IMPLEMENTATION STRATEGIES

In the European countries visited, the general philosophy for roadway design and project development is to develop a transportation program and system that enhances community values and integrates roadways into communities and the environment. This philosophy permeates their project development process, safety improvements, roadway design concepts, geometric design guidelines, public involvement, and environmental commitments. This same philosophy is the essence of the recent push to promote the CSD approach in the United States, a shift that is supported by FHWA and many State DOTs. The design philosophy of the Europeans is to develop a roadway that is designed for a specific purpose, implements an aesthetic approach to visually explain this concept, and addresses safety in a way that considers all users. Finally, all countries have very high safety goals (ranging from zero fatalities to reductions of more than 40 percent in all crashes), which guide their design approach and philosophy. To achieve these goals the Europeans are willing to provide roadways that self-enforce speed limits, potentially increase levels of congestion, and promote alternative modes of transportation. This approach contrasts with the U.S. design philosophy, in which wider roads are deemed safer, there is a heavier reliance on signs to communicate the intended message, and there is a lower tolerance of congestion and speed reduction.

The visits to these five countries exposed the panel to a variety of practices and programs that may be transferable to specific locations and situations in the United States. A wide variety of practices was found among the agencies of these countries that stem from differences such as size, population, safety goals, and general design philosophy. Although all practices are not entirely new to all States in the United States, we may be able to learn from their form and the extent of their application in Europe. Therefore, each U.S. agency should evaluate the application and use of the ideas presented in both the previous and this section. To this end, the U.S. scan team has developed the following list of implementation strategies for enhancing existing project development and roadway geometric design practices in the United States.

PROJECT PLANNING

A practice common in all five countries visited was the longer period of time devoted to the planning process and the consideration of longer sections, typically entire corridors. This is an approach some agencies may want to consider, since it provides the opportunity for long-range planning by allowing for a more systematic overview and for defining needs and deficiencies over the entire system. The greater emphasis in urban areas on integrating projects in communities by addressing the public's concerns for speed management and aesthetics is an additional area that State and local agencies may consider while developing projects.

All five countries involve the public in most projects and involve a variety of other stakeholders depending on the project type and stage. Early public involvement is considered a significant means for decreasing project times and resolving potential conflicts in early stages of the project. The participation of local agencies in this process and their ability to control decisions in certain projects is an aspect that merits further consideration. Such local agencies may be capable of addressing specific needs and local concerns more appropriately than State agencies and, thus, their participation is often beneficial in developing a project that is responsive to local needs. Involvement of the public and appropriate stakeholders at the earliest possible stage of the project enables a successful project that addresses their concerns. This concept could be applied in the United States not only to reduce the project times by minimizing conflicts but also to improve relationships between State agencies and the public by developing a constructive dialogue.

The Dutch are using a process of design workshops in which all project alternatives are developed with public involvement. This process seems to alleviate conflicts between highway agencies and the public and reduces project planning time by resolving issues in the early stages of the project. This system merits additional examination and could be transferable to the United States.

RURAL ROADS

The concept of 2+1 roads has been shown to simultaneously address safety and capacity issues on two-lane roadways. This design is more economical than conversion to four-lane roadways and, thus, is considered an applicable concept. This design is similar to the U.S. practice of providing passing lanes on two-lane roads. However, specific design elements for successful implementation need to be specified and design guidelines for their implementation need to be developed. Morever, some safety concerns still exist among the Europeans, and these issues need to be examined prior to adopting this design.

Another concept that could benefit the United States is the concept of self-explaining, self-enforcing roads. Such roads are designed for a specific purpose or function and they address safety in an efficient way for all users by implementing an aesthetic approach to explain the road function and enforce speeds. This is the ultimate goal of a roadway design, since roadways designed this way meet drivers' expectations rather than surprise them. Reliance on the roadway design to transmit its operating speed is integral to this concept and conflicting messages should be avoided. The higher reliance in the United States on traffic signs to convey the desired operating speeds may create additional problems, since often there are conflicting messages between the traffic signs and the roadway image. It is reasonable to examine these possible conflicts and evaluate whether the wider roadway widths that have been utilized in the United States are more conducive to crashes by encouraging the driver to drive at inappropriate speeds.

TRAFFIC CALMING

Traffic calming is an effective means for controlling speeds through urban areas and deserves wider implementation in the United States. A variety of components are available with different uses, applications, and effectiveness. All studies completed indicate that, indeed, these devices do reduce speeds at a variety of levels. Traffic calming is most effective if done on a neighborhood or area-wide basis and not just at spot locations. While some of the measures have been tried to a limited degree in the United States, more testing of various European traffic calming strategies is needed in U.S. cities. Reliance on speed limit and STOP signs and police enforcement does not fully achieve the desired speed reductions, since the roadways are not conveying the intended message and are not forcing the driver to slow down. Use of these designs also reduces the need for police enforcement efforts.

ROUNDABOUTS

Roundabouts are a very safe and efficient means for intersection control. Roundabouts with a single-lane approach are used widely and successfully in Europe and they can easily accommodate peak flows of 2,500 vehicles per hour without significant delays. Roundabouts with two approach lanes are widely used in England but are being introduced more cautiously in continental Europe because of concerns about driver confusion and safety. Safety studies completed in most of these countries indicate that significant safety gains were achieved by implementing roundabouts in place of conventional intersections. (It should be noted that the studies conducted in continental Europe predominantly relate to single-lane roundabouts, not necessarily to roundabouts in general.) Although roundabouts have been introduced in a few areas in the United States, this modern tool is still underutilized. State and local agencies should consider the implementation and use of roundabouts as an alternative to conventional intersection designs as well as a means for improving traffic safety. When roundabouts are introduced for the first time in a community, they should be placed in areas where single-lane approaches would accommodate the existing traffic. This approach will ensure the successful and smooth operation of the site and, thus, promote the use of this alternative design.

BICYCLISTS AND PEDESTRIANS

All countries visited place significant emphasis on addressing the needs of pedestrians and bicyclists. Bicycle networks exist in all countries; in some they are complete and rival the vehicle networks. For some countries addressing the needs of these users is as important as improving vehicle mobility, and promoting use of bicycles as an alternative mode of transport is a strong commitment of the highway agencies. A change in philosophy is needed in the United States to focus directly on promoting use of bicycles and other transport modes in conjunction with automobile travel. Addressing mobility needs has been viewed traditionally in the United States as providing a roadway network in which drivers can move as quickly and freely as they desire. This notion needs to be altered in order to address the safety needs of vulnerable road users. State and local agencies should focus on providing bicycle and pedestrian networks, since they are essential in promoting use of these modes of transport. A lesson learned from the scan tour was that a high level of commitment is essential in promoting bicycle usage, and a systematic accommodation is required to increase use of alternative modes of transport. Completion of existing networks is also central to a successful campaign. Morever, zoning and development practices may need to be revisited to create an environment to promote biking and walking in urban centers.

CONTEXT-SENSITIVE DESIGN

All countries visited follow the practice of developing transportation projects and systems that enhance community values while integrating roadways into the environment. Several agencies employ the use of multi-disciplinary teams to develop design solutions, which allows them to approach problems from several possible angles. Such an approach considers and addresses all phases of the project when appropriate and thus reduces project time and possible costs. Moreover, consideration is given to the desires and needs of the community by inviting the appropriate stakeholders to participate in the development of the project and thus shape some of the solutions that are acceptable to the community. This approach is currently promoted by FHWA and AASHTO and it should be continued in the future until it becomes an integral part of the design process in the United States Although not unheard of in the United States, design solutions that reduce motor vehicle speeds or reduce the space available to vehicles may increase trip times and are not often viewed as appropriate. But wider, high-speed roads that address only the mobility needs of automobile users may not meet the needs of other users of the transportation system. Most often design solutions seek to reduce delays to motorists at all costs. Such road designs encourage higher travel speeds that contribute to greater severity of crashes. These are important aspects of applying the concepts of CSD, since community desires may conflict with high-speed designs.

CSD implies a flexible application of the established geometric criteria in designing roadways. The use of innovative design to address local problems and provide solutions within the context of the area is essential in applying the CSD concept. The self-enforcing, self-explaining road is an example of such innovative design, since it encourages lower operating speeds for automobiles while incorporating safety and mobility for all transport modes. To facilitate this flexibility, some countries explicitly indicate that deviations from their design manuals are accepted and provide reasons and situations in which such changes are appropriate. In addition, documentation exists that describes the appropriate supportive documents to justify these deviations. Consequently, the Europeans use design exceptions to address CSD concepts and they use aesthetics both for safety enforcement and visual appeal.

IMPLEMENTATION STRATEGY

A summary of proposed activities and implementation strategies for each of the findings discussed here is presented in Table 5.

Table 5. Summary of findings and implementation strategies.

Subject	Recommendations and implementation strategies
Project Planning	• Investigate the Dutch use of design workshops to determine whether this practice can enhance the CSD approach and improve and expedite the existing NEPA process. Consider piloting studies, if appropriate.
	• Encourage States to consider including public involvement in the earliest possible stage of the project planning process.

Subject	Recommendations and implementation strategies
2+1 Roads	• Survey existing practices in the EU and the United States and develop a Synthesis Report sponsored by TRB. The Task Force on Geometric design of AASHTO will develop a proposal for TRB.
Geometric Design Philosophy	• Increase awareness among practitioners and roadway designers, possibly through an educational effort sponsored by AASHTO, TRB, and APWA.
Roundabouts	• Encourage States to consider initial implementation of roundabouts at areas where success is guaranteed. • Initiate an educational campaign to promote use of roundabouts in the United States by developing a workshop and inviting European experts. Several agencies and professional organizations could sponsor this, including FHWA, AASHTO, APWA, ASCE, and ITE. • Form a steering committee to determine an educational strategy. • Increase dissemination of the report *Roundabouts: An Information Guide*, FHWA-RD-00-067.
Traffic Calming	• Identify and document available literature regarding traffic calming practices, possibly through a Synthesis Report sponsored by APWA, TRB, or ITE. • Initiate a professional awareness campaign to promote proper use of traffic calming devices through an APWA information campaign. • Support development of an APWA informational document on the use of traffic calming devices. • Develop a course or workshop proposal on use of traffic calming devices. This is a possible followup action item for FHWA and AASHTO.
Context Sensitive Design	• Promote the development of a workshop or course that addresses CSD concepts to be delivered nationwide. • Make short presentations on the CSD philosophy, including aesthetics, traffic calming, self-explaining self-enforcing roads, and roundabouts at various meetings: AASHTO, FHWA, ASCE, and ITE. • Identify courses offered by the National Highway Institute (NHI) that need to be updated to include CSD concepts. • Promote CSD concepts to impact high-level personnel of highway agencies and academia.

REFERENCES

1. Federal Highway Administration, 1997. *Flexibility in Highway Design*, FHWA-PD-97-062, Washington, D.C.

2. Swedish National Road Administration, 2000. *Facts About the Swedish National Road Administration, Roads and Traffic.* Publication 2000:23E, Borlange, Sweden.

3. Swedish National Road Administration, 1998. *1997 Road Traffic Safety Report*, Publication 1998:20, Borlange, Sweden.

4. Road Directorate, 1998. *Research and Development: Road Safety and Environment*, Copenhagen, Denmark.

5. Nielsen, M.A., Lund, B., and Nielsen, E.D. 1998. *Accidents on Rural Roads in Denmark*, Note No. 50, Road Directorate, Copenhagen, Denmark.

6. Schermers, G. 1999. *Sustainable Safety: A Preventive Road Safety Strategy for the Future*, Transport Research Center, Ministry of Transport and Public Works, Rotterdam, The Netherlands.

7. Highways Agency, 1999. *Highways Agency Business Plan 1999/2000*, London, England.

8. Highways Agency, 2000. *Making the Network Safer*, London, England.

9. Highways Agency, 2000. *Towards a Balance with Nature*, London, England.

10. Kjemtrup, K. 1999. *Guidelines for Geometric Design of Roads and Paths in Urban Areas*, Danish Road Directorate, Copenhagen, Denmark.

11. Forschungsgesellgesahftfur Strassen und Verkehrswesen (FGSV), 1988. *Guidelines for the Construction of Roads, Part: Manual for the Functional Structuring of the Road System, RAS-N*, Kirschbaum Verlag, Bonn, Germany.

12. Department of Transport, 1993. *Design Manual for Roads and Bridges, Road Geometry, Links, Part 1*, TD 9/93, Highway Link Design, England.

13. Highways Agency, 1999. *Procedures Manual, Vol. 2, Procedures for Departures from Standards*, London, England.

14. Herrstedt, L., Kjemtrup, K., Borges, P., and Andersen, P. 1993. *An Improved Traffic Environment, A Catalogue of Ideas*, Road Standards Division Report 106, Road Directorate, Copenhagen, Denmark.

15. Greibe, P. and Nilsson, P. 1999. *Speed Management, National Practice and Experience in Denmark, the Netherlands and in the United Kingdom*, Report No. 167, Road Directorate, Copenhagen, Denmark.

16. Greibe, P., Nilsson, P., and Herrstedt, L. 1999. *Speed Management in Urban Areas, A Framework for the Planning and Evaluation Process*, Report No. 168, Road Directorate, Copenhagen, Denmark.

17. Department of the Environment, 1999. *Traffic Calming Bibliography*, Traffic Advisory Leaflet 4/99, London, England.

18. Wheeler, A. and Taylor, M., 2000. *Changes in Accident Frequency Following the Introduction of Traffic Calming in Villages,* TRL Report 452, Transport Research Laboratory, London, England.

19. Kjemtrup, K. 1988. Speed Reducing Measures. *Australian Road Research Board* Proceedings, Vol. 14, Part 2, Canberra, Australia.

20. Department of Transport, 1993. *Design Manual for Roads and Bridges, Road Geometry, Junctions, Part 3,* TD16/93; TD 78/97; TD 50/99, England.

21. Forschungsgesellgesahftfur Strassen und Verkehrswesen (FGSV), 1988. *Guidelines for the Construction of Roads, Part: Nodal Points, Section 1: Flat Nodal Points, RAS-K-1,* Kirschbaum Verlag, Bonn, Germany.

22. Road Directorate, 1993. *Urban Traffic Areas, Part 4 Intersections,* Copenhagen, Denmark.

23. Centrum fur Regelgeving en Onderzoek in de Grond-, Water-, en Wegenbouw en de Verkeerstechniek (CROW), *Eenheid in Rotondes (Uniformity in Roundabouts),* CROW Publications 126, EDE, The Netherlands, 1998.

24. Centrum for Regelgeving en Onderzoek in de Grond-, Water-, en Wegenbouw en de Verkeerstechniek (CROW), *ASVV –Aanbevelingen voor Verkeersvoorzieningen binnen debebouwde kom (Recommendations for Traffic Facilities in Urban Areas),* CROW Publications 110, EDE, The Netherlands, 1996.

25. Swedish Association of Local Authorities, 1999. *Calm Streets,* Stockholm, Sweden.

26. Road Directorate, 1998. *Best Practice to Promote Cycling and Walking-ADONIS ,* Copenhagen, Denmark.

Appendix A

Team Members

Addresses at the time of scan tour

Dr. Kam Movassaghi (Co-Chair)
Secretary
Louisiana Department of
    Transportation
P.O. Box 94245
1201 Capitol Access Road
Baton Rouge, LA 70804-9245
Tel: (225) 379-1200
Fax: (225) 379-1851
E-mail:
kkm@dotdmail.dotd.state.la.us

Sandra Otto (Co-Chair)
Assistant Division Administrator
FHWA Arkansas Division
700 West Capitol Avenue (Room 3130)
Little Rock, AR 72201-3298
Tel: (501) 324-6436/5625
Fax: (501) 324-6423
E-mail: **sandra.otto@fhwa.dot.gov**

Jim Brewer
Engineering Manager - State Road
    Office
Kansas DOT
9th Floor Docking State Office Bldg.
Topeka, KS 66612
Tel: (785) 296 3901
Fax: (785) 296-6946
E-mail: **jbrewer@ksdot.org**

John German
Public Works Director
City of San Antonio
P.O. Box 839966
San Antonio, TX 78283-3966
Tel: (210) 207-8023
Fax: (210) 207-4406
E-mail: **jgerman@ci.sat.tx.us**

Ray Krammes
Senior Highway Research Engineer
FHWA, Turner-Fairbank Highway
    Research Center
(HRDS-05)
6300 Georgetown Pike
McLean, VA 22101
Tel: (202) 493-3312
Fax: (202) 493-3417
E-mail: **ray.krammes@fhwa.dot.gov**

John Okamoto
Regional Administrator
Northwest Region
Washington Department of
    Transportation
P.O. Box 330310
Seattle, WA 98133-9710
Tel: (206) 440-4691/4690
Fax: (206) 440-4808
E-mail: **okamoto@wsdot.wa.gov**

Wendell Ruff
Assistant Chief Engineer
Mississippi Department of
    Transportation
Administrative Office Building
P.O. Box 1850
401 North West Street
Jackson, MS 39215-1850
Tel: (601) 359-7007
Fax: (601) 359-7050
E-mail: **wruff@mdot.state.ms.us**

Seppo Sillan
Senior Engineer-Design
FHWA Office of Program
    Administration
Infrastructure Core Business Unit
(HIPA-20) (Room 3134)
400 Seventh Street, S.W.
Washington, DC 20590
Tel:(202) 366-1327
Fax:(202) 366-3988
E-mail: **seppo.sillan@fhwa.dot.gov**

Nick Stamatiadis (Report Facilitator)
Associate Professor of Civil
Engineering
    Transportation
265 Raymond Building
University of Kentucky
Lexington, KY 40506-0281
Tel:(606) 257-8012
Fax:(606) 257-4404
E-mail: **nstamat@pop.engr.uky.edu**

Bob Walters
Chief Engineer
Arkansas Highway & Transportation
    Department
P.O. Box 2261
Little Rock, AR 72203
Tel:(501) 569-2214
Fax:(501) 569-2688
E-mail: **rlwe158@ahtd.state.ar.us**

BIOGRAPHIC SKETCHES

Dr. Kam Movassaghi, Panel Co-Chair, is Secretary of the Department of Transportation and Development in the State of Louisiana (LADOTD) with headquarters in Baton Rouge, Louisiana. Dr. Movassaghi currently directs a staff of 5,600 employees and an annual budget of more than $1 billion. LADOTD's scope of operation includes all modes of transportation in addition to ports, flood control, water resources, and an offshore oil terminal. The Department's research activities are housed at the Louisiana Transportation Research Center, located on the Louisiana State University campus and supported by LADOTD. Prior to joining LADOTD in 1998, he served as professor and head of the Department of Civil Engineering at the University of Louisiana in Lafayette. His research areas of interest included transportation planning and operations, GIS-T, and network analysis and logistics. Dr. Movassaghi is a graduate of the University of Louisiana in Lafayette and holds a Master's degree and a Ph.D. in Civil Engineering from Louisiana State University. He is a licensed professional engineer in Louisiana and has served on several technical and professional committees of the American Society of Civil Engineers. Currently, he is president of the Southeastern Association of State Highway and Transportation Officials and a member of the Executive Committee of the American Association of State Highway and Transportation Officials.

Sandra Otto, Panel Co-Chair, is the Assistant Division Administrator (ADA) for the Arkansas Division of the U.S. Federal Highway Administration (FHWA). As ADA, Ms. Otto shares responsibility with the Division Administrator for administering the Federal-aid highway program in Arkansas. This includes ensuring that FHWA emphasis areas, including context-sensitive highway design, are advanced within the State of Arkansas. This past year, as Chair of the American Society of Civil Engineers' (ASCE) Environmental Quality Committee, she was responsible for presenting a nationwide workshop on Context Sensitive Highway Design in the Washington, D.C., area. Prior to her promotion to ADA, Ms. Otto was Program Development Engineer in the Colorado Division and a Special Assistant to the Environmental Operations Division Chief in Washington, D.C. Ms. Otto holds a Bachelor of Science degree in Civil Engineering from Montana State University and a Master's in Environmental Management and Public Policy (MPA) from The George Washington University. She is a licensed professional engineer in Washington and current Chair of the ASCE Highway Division's Environmental Quality Committee.

James O. (Jim) Brewer is the Engineering Manager of the State Road Office for the Kansas Department of Transportation (KDOT) in Topeka, Kansas. He manages the pre-construction portion of KDOT's $12.9 billion, 10-year Comprehensive Transportation Program, which includes all location studies and geometric design. He has been with KDOT for 33 years with more than 30 years of that time involved in road design. He graduated from the University of Arkansas with a Bachelor of Science degree in Civil Engineering. He is a registered professional engineer in Kansas. He serves on the American Association of State Highway and Transportation Officials (AASHTO) Task Forces on Geometric Design and Aesthetic Design. He also has served on several technical committees of the Transportation Research Board. In addition, Mr. Brewer currently is a member of the AASHTO Subcommittee on Design.

John L. German is the Director of Public Works for the City of San Antonio, Texas, and is currently responsible for more than 1,600 employees, an operating budget of $106 million, and a $300 million capital improvement program of which $85 million is expended in the current budget. Functions under his direction include streets and drainage maintenance and operations, solid waste and environmental services, building construction and maintenance, capital projects management, engineering, traffic operations, and parking for a city with a population greater than 1 million. Prior to his current position, Mr. German was President and Chief Executive Officer of the Texas Research and Development Foundation and was also a Senior Traffic Engineering Consultant (1988-92). In this position he was project manager for the Long-term Pavement Performance research project under the Strategic Highway Program. He also has served as Executive Vice President for Land Development with Franklin Savings in Austin (1983-88), and Director of Public Works and as Assistant City Manager for the City of Austin, Texas, between 1977-1983. He held other positions in traffic engineering, transportation planning, and geometric design prior to these assignments. Mr. German is a graduate of Texas A&M University with a Bachelor's degree in Civil Engineering and the Yale University Bureau of Highway Traffic with the Master's equivalent in Traffic Engineering and Transportation Planning. He also holds a Master's of Public Administration degree from the Lyndon Baines Johnson School of Public Affairs at the University of Texas. He is a licensed professional engineer in the State of Texas, is a Fellow of the Institute of Transportation Engineers (ITE), and an active member of the American Public Works Association, the American Society of Civil

Engineers, and the American Society of Testing and Materials. He also serves as the Chair of the Governmental Affairs Committee and as a member of the Engineering and Technology Committee of the American Public Works Association. He previously served on various ITE committees dealing with geometric design issues. Mr. German is well qualified to represent cities on this scanning tour, having served as an officer of many professional organizations, written numerous articles, and spoken on a wide variety of technical and management issues during his 33 years of professional service.

Dr. Ray Krammes is a senior highway research engineer for the U.S. Federal Highway Administration (FHWA). Dr. Krammes is Roadway Team Leader in FHWA's Office of Safety Research and Development at the Turner-Fairbank Highway Research Center in McLean, Virginia. The Roadway Team develops geometric-design, speed-management, and visibility-enhancement techniques and safety evaluation tools to keep vehicles on the roadway, decrease speed-related causes of crashes, improve pedestrian and bicyclist safety, and make highway work zones safer. Dr. Krammes manages development of the Interactive Highway Safety Design Model, a suite of software analysis tools for quantitative evaluation of the safety impacts of highway geometric design decisions. Prior to joining FHWA in 1997, Dr. Krammes was on the Civil Engineering faculty at Texas A&M University and conducted traffic engineering research through the Texas Transportation Institute. He received his B.S., M.S., and Ph.D. in Civil Engineering from The Pennsylvania State University. He serves on geometric-design related technical committees of the American Society of Civil Engineers, Institute of Transportation Engineers, and the Transportation Research Board.

John Okamoto is Regional Administrator for the Washington State Department of Transportation. As Regional Administrator, Mr. Okamoto is responsible for planning, designing, construction, and operation of interstate and State highways in the most populated region in the State with more than 2.5 million residents. He is responsible for coordinating transportation services with local governments, marine and air port authorities, public transit agencies, rail operators, and the nation's largest public ferry system. Mr. Okamoto's region employs 1,600 employees with a biennial budget of $1.1 billion. Prior to being appointed as Regional Administrator, Mr. Okamoto spent nearly 20 years with the City of Seattle serving in several department-head positions, including Director of Engineering. He has a Bachelor's degree and a Master's degree in public administration from the University of Washington, and has attended Harvard University's John F. Kennedy School of Government. Mr. Okamoto has served on many national and State transportation committees, and is current transportation chair of the American Public Works Association.

Wendell T. Ruff is the Assistant Chief Engineer for the Mississippi Department of Transportation (MDOT) at State headquarters in Jackson, Mississippi. He currently directs the Department's Pre-construction Engineering Activities. His duties include oversight of roadway and bridge design, environmental/location activities, right-of-way acquisition, and research. Prior to being appointed Assistant Chief Engineer in 1998, he served as the Roadway Design Division Engineer and the State Geotechnical Engineer for MDOT. Mr. Ruff is a graduate of Mississippi State University and holds a Bachelor's degree in Civil Engineering. He is a licensed professional engineer in Mississippi and serves on several technical committees of the American Association of State Highway and Transportation Officials and the Transportation Research Board.

Seppo I. Sillan is the Senior Engineer, Office of Program Administration of the U.S. Federal Highway Administration (FHWA) in Washington, D.C. His current responsibilities include directing the development, implementation, and monitoring of national highway geometric design standards, policies and guidelines, value engineering program, and pre-construction procedures such as use of consultants. His past positions include division, region and headquarters office assignments in design, construction, maintenance, research, and technology transfer areas. Prior to joining the FHWA he worked with the California Highway Department. He obtained his Bachelor's degree in Civil Engineering from the University of Florida. Mr. Sillan is active in various committees and task forces of the American Association of State Highway and Transportation Officials, the American Society of Civil Engineers, and the Transportation Research Board. He is also an active member of the World Road Association Committee on Roads, Transport and Regional Development.

Dr. Nikiforos Stamatiadis, the Report Facilitator, is an Associate Professor of Civil Engineering at the University of Kentucky (UK) in Lexington, Kentucky. At UK he teaches transportation and traffic-related courses and he supervises and conducts transportation engineering research with an emphasis on human factors, traffic safety, and geometric design. His current research emphasis includes the impact of context-sensitive designs on safety, development of relationships between crashes on rural roads and geometric features, evaluation of driver licensing renewal procedures, and safety concerns for elderly drivers. Prior to joining the faculty at UK in 1990, he worked as a full-time researcher at Michigan State University, East Lansing, Michigan, and Aristotle University of Thessaloniki, Thessaloniki, Greece. Dr. Stamatiadis holds a Bachelor's degree in Surveying Engineering from Aristotle University of Thessaloniki, and M.S. and Ph.D. degrees in Civil Engineering from Michigan State University. He is a licensed professional engineer in Michigan, Kentucky, Indiana, and Europe, and serves on several technical committees of the American Society of Civil Engineers, the Institute of Transportation Engineers, and the Transportation Research Board. Dr. Stamatiadis is also the president of the Kentucky Section of the Institute of Transportation Engineers.

Robert (Bob) Walters is the Chief Engineer for the Arkansas Highway and Transportation Department in Little Rock, Arkansas. He has worked for the Arkansas Highway and Transportation Department for 28 years, with 26 years in the highway design area. As Chief Engineer, he now oversees planning, design, construction, and maintenance of the State's highway system. Mr. Walters is a graduate of the University of Arkansas with a Bachelor's and a Master's degree in Civil Engineering. He is a licensed professional engineer in Arkansas. He is a past Vice-Chair of the American Association of State Highway and Transportation Officials' (AASHTO's) Joint Task Force on Pavements, and currently serves as the Chair of the AASHTO Task Force on Geometric Design. This Task Force is charged with updating the AASHTO "Policy on Geometric Design of Highways and Streets." In addition, Mr. Walters is currently serving as a member of the National Cooperative Highway Research Program Panel researching design speed and operating speed issues.

APPENDIX B

AMPLIFYING QUESTIONS

The following is a list of questions on six areas that the U.S. panel would like to discuss with you. These questions are intended to clarify and expand on the Panel Topics of Interest described in the Panel Overview paper. The questions are arranged by topic and the questions are grouped based on major concepts within each of the six areas. At the end of each theme, a general category attempts to further define some of the concepts asked in the previous groups and elaborate on some very specific topics of these questions.

The panel is very interested in being able to visit sites where some of the concepts discussed have been applied. If possible, the panel would like to be able to devote 50 percent or more of its time with you for site visits. Examples of successful and not-so-successful applications are of interest to the panel to allow for a broader understanding of these topics.

I. Context-Sensitive Design (CSD) and Project Development Procedures and Practices

*Context-sensitive design is a term being used in the United States for the project development process, including geometric design, which is responsive to or consistent with the road's natural and human environment.

Project Development

1. What are the typical steps in your project development process? Describe your procedures for initiating, defining, and fully developing projects from conception through the design stage.

2. What role does public involvement play in project development? Collaborative decision making (road type and character, design aspects, etc.) or in an advisory capacity only? How are outside stakeholders identified?

Design Issues

3. What document establishes your prevailing national design criteria?

4. What are the safety results of road designs that use geometric features to control speed or designs that reduce space for vehicles in order to accommodate other modes of transport, especially pedestrians and bicyclists?

Context-Sensitive Design

5. When it becomes necessary to deviate from the accepted design criteria in order to accommodate environmental, historic, or other cultural values and/or other modes of transportation, what is the most common geometric design element involved in context-sensitive considerations (lane width, speed, horizontal curvature, etc.)?

6. What are the liability issues associated with such deviations from the accepted criteria?

Other

7. How are tradeoffs made throughout the project development process among environmental impacts, community values, construction cost, and safety?

8. How does your planning staff, environmental staff, and design staff coordinate to ensure that decisions made at one stage are passed on to the next?

9. How are environmental considerations and community values factored into your project development procedures and practices?

10. What special rules, if any, are applied to road projects that are in environmentally or aesthetically sensitive, or historically and/or culturally important areas?

11. Does your agency have additional guidelines to address flexibility for accommodating scenic, historic, cultural, or otherwise important or critical aspects impacted by the road project?

12. How are policy decisions made about flexing design criteria to fit the context of the current project?

II. Design and Operating Speed in Geometric Design

Design Speed

13. How does your agency define design speed?

14. How is the design speed selected for a project, i.e., what factors are considered in selecting the design speed?

Operating Speed

15. How, if at all, is anticipated operating speed used in geometric design?

16. Do your design procedures include evaluating the uniformity, or consistency, of the expected operating speeds along rural highway projects?

Speed Limit

17. Does the posted speed ever exceed the design speed? If so, has this created any safety or other problems and how do you address them?

Design Issues

18. Are specific design measures employed to keep speeds at certain levels (for instance, introducing horizontal curvature to eliminate long tangent sections or use of alignment and/or cross-section design to control actual operating speeds)?

19. Do you use speed or a non-speed-related method, such as functional classification or "design class," to determine geometric elements?

III. Design Solutions for High-Volume Rural Highways

Planning Issues

20. How do you balance the need for mobility on high-volume rural highways with safety for bicyclists and pedestrians?

21. Is access control a factor? If so, how?

Alternatives

22. What design alternatives are considered for improving high-volume two-lane rural highways without going to a four-lane section? What has been your safety and operational experience with these alternatives?

IV. Roundabouts

23. What is your experience with safety and operations (for motorists, pedestrians, and bicyclists) at modern roundabouts in urban and rural areas of your country?

Design Issues

24. Does your agency have specific design guidelines for roundabouts?

Operation Issues

25. Where do roundabouts work well and where not?

26. At what traffic levels do you consider roundabouts ineffective or inappropriate?

V. Speed-Moderating Techniques on Rural Roads (Especially Through Towns)

Design Philosophy

27. What design strategies are used to reduce speeds on primary rural roads approaching and through towns?

Other

28. What kinds of transition techniques are employed between the higher-speed rural and lower-speed urban areas?

29. What is your experience with signing, enforcement, speed bumps, and use of alternate roadway sections as means for moderating speeds through towns?

VI. Accommodations for Vulnerable Users Such as Pedestrians and Bicyclists

Design Philosophy

30. How are tradeoffs among pedestrian, bicyclist, and motorist safety and mobility considered in project development and design?

Other

31. What have been your most successful accommodations to improve pedestrian and bicyclist safety on rural highways? At roundabouts? At other intersection types? On main urban streets? On urban residential streets? On highway interchanges?

32. What is the typical modal split (passenger vehicles, commercial vehicles, pedestrians, bicyclists) on your rural highways, main urban streets, and urban residential streets?

33. How do these splits affect your choice for providing bike/pedestrian facilities?

34. Do you provide bike/pedestrian accommodation on all public roadways? If not, on what types of roads?

APPENDIX C

EUROPEAN CONTACTS

Sweden

Torsten Bergh, M.Sc., C.E.
Road Design & Traffic Engineer
  Specialist
Road & Traffic Management Division
Swedish National Road Administration
S-781 87 Borlange, Sweden
E-mail: **torsten.bergh@vv.se**

Denmark

Lene Herrstedt, M.Sc., Ph.D.
Head of Research Division
Traffic Safety and Environment
Road Directorate
Niels Juels Gade 13
Postboks 1569
DK-1059 Copenhagen K, Denmark
E-mail: **leh@vd.dk**

The Netherlands

Govert Schermers
Senior Consultant Traffic Safety
Department for Transport and Society
Transport Research Centre (AVV)
Ministry of Transport, Public Works
  and Water Management
Boompes 200
P.O. Box 1031
3000 BA Rotterdam, The Netherlands
E-mail:
g.schermers@avv.rws.minvenw.nl

England

John Smart, B.Sc. Ceng MICE
Principal Technical Advisor (Safety)
Room 4/36, St. Christopher House
Southwark Street
London SE1 0TE, United Kingdom
E-mail:
john.smart@highways.gsi.gov.uk

Germany

Dr.-Ing. Karl F. Ribbeck
Roads Directorate-General
Division International Cooperation
Research and Development
Robert Schuman Platz 1
D-53175, Bonn
E-mail:
Karl.Ribbeck@bmvbw.bund.de

FHWA INTERNATIONAL TECHNOLOGY EXCHANGE REPORTS

Infrastructure

Geotechnical Engineering Practices in Canada and Europe✓⊕
Geotechnology—Soil Nailing✓⊕
International Contract Administration Techniques for Quality Enhancement-CATQEST✓⊕

Pavements

European Asphalt Technology✓⊕✓⊕
European Concrete Technology✓⊕✓⊕
South African Pavement Technology
Highway Information Management
Highway/Commercial Vehicle Interaction

Bridges

European Bridge Structures
Asian Bridge Structures
Bridge Maintenance Coatings
European Practices for Bridge Scour and Stream Instability Countermeasures
Advanced Composites in Bridges in Europe and Japan✓⊕
Steel Bridge Fabrication Technologies in Europe and Japan✓⊕
Performance of Concrete Segmental and Cable-Stayed Bridges in Europe✓⊕

Planning and Environment

European Intermodal Programs: Planning, Policy and Technology✓⊕
National Travel Surveys✓⊕
Recycled Materials in European Highway Environments✓⊕

Safety

Pedestrian and Bicycle Safety in England, Germany and the Netherlands✓⊕
Speed Management and Enforcement Technology: Europe & Australia✓⊕
Safety Management Practices in Japan, Australia, and New Zealand✓⊕
Road Safety Audits—Final Report✓⊕
Road Safety Audits—Case Studies✓⊕
Innovative Traffic Control Technology & Practice in Europe✓⊕
Commercial Vehicle Safety Technology & Practice in Europe✓⊕

Operations

Advanced Transportation Technology✓⊕
European Traffic Monitoring
Traffic Management and Traveler Information Systems
European Winter Service Technology
Snowbreak Forest Book – Highway Snowstorm Countermeasure Manual (*Translated from Japanese*)

Policy & Information

Emerging Models for Delivering Transportation Programs and Services
Acquiring Highway Transportation Information from Abroad—Handbook✓⊕
Acquiring Highway Transportation Information from Abroad—Final Report✓⊕
International Guide to Highway Transportation Information✓⊕

✓⊕**Also available on the internet**
✓⊕✓⊕**Only on the internet at www.international.fhwa.dot.gov**

NOTES

NOTES

www.ingramcontent.com/pod-product-compliance
Lightning Source LLC
Chambersburg PA
CBHW080906290526
45795CB00007BA/2433